AF262847

BROWNSVILLE TO BRADDOCK

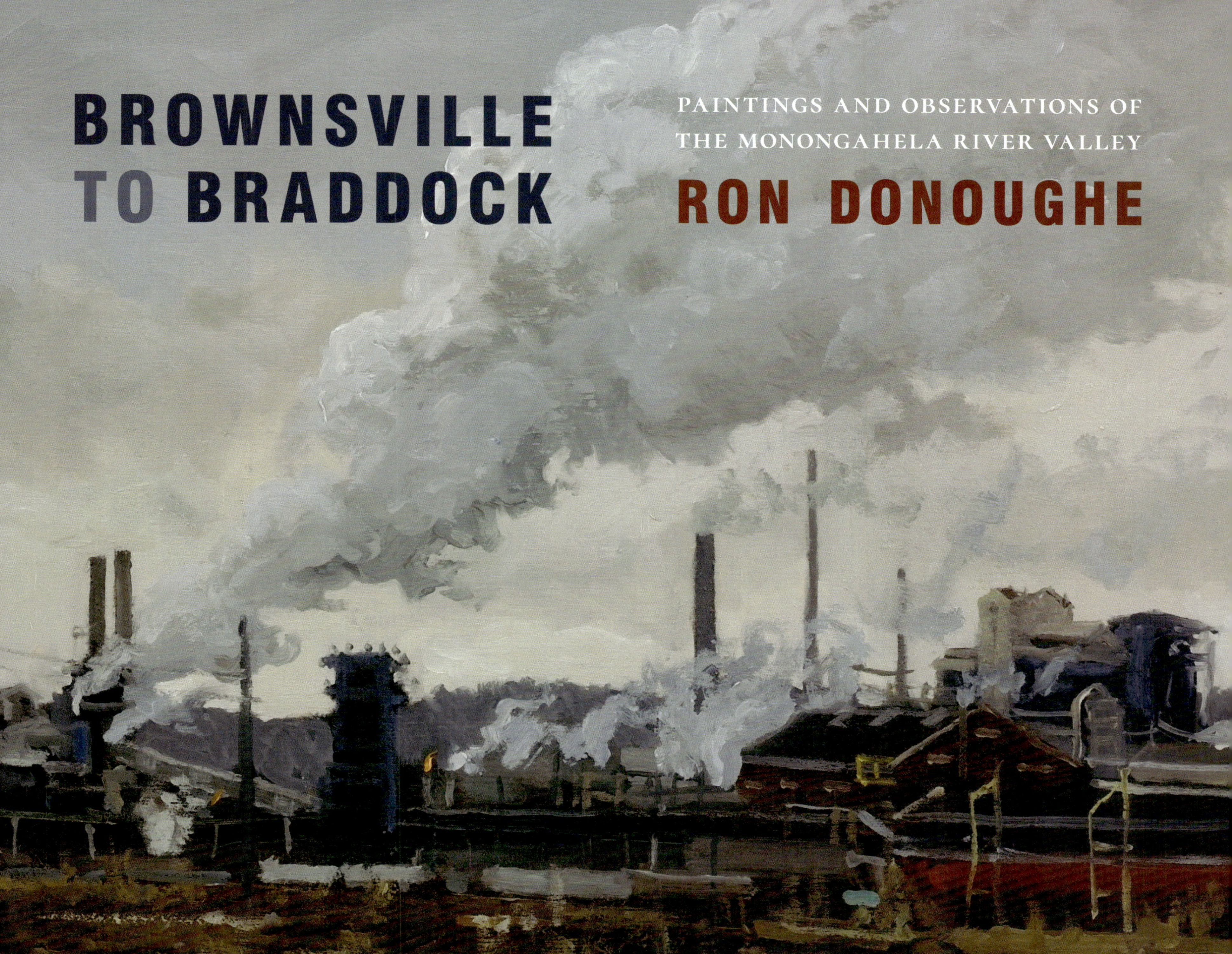

BROWNSVILLE TO BRADDOCK
PAINTINGS AND OBSERVATIONS OF THE MONONGAHELA RIVER VALLEY
RON DONOUGHE

This publication is made possible through the generous support of
The Robert S. Waters Fund at the Pittsburgh Foundation

Published by the University of Pittsburgh Press, Pittsburgh, Pa., 15260
Copyright © 2021, University of Pittsburgh Press

Manufactured in Canada
Printed on acid-free paper
10 9 8 7 6 5 4 3 2 1

Cataloging-in-Publication data is available from the Library of Congress

ISBN 13: 978-0-8229-4675-5
ISBN 10: 0-8229-4675-0

COVER ART: Ron Donoughe, *Clairton Plumes*
COVER DESIGN: Alex Wolfe

To my mother, Camilla—

An orphan, an independent thinker, a mother of ten,
and a product of the Mon Valley, although she didn't even know it.

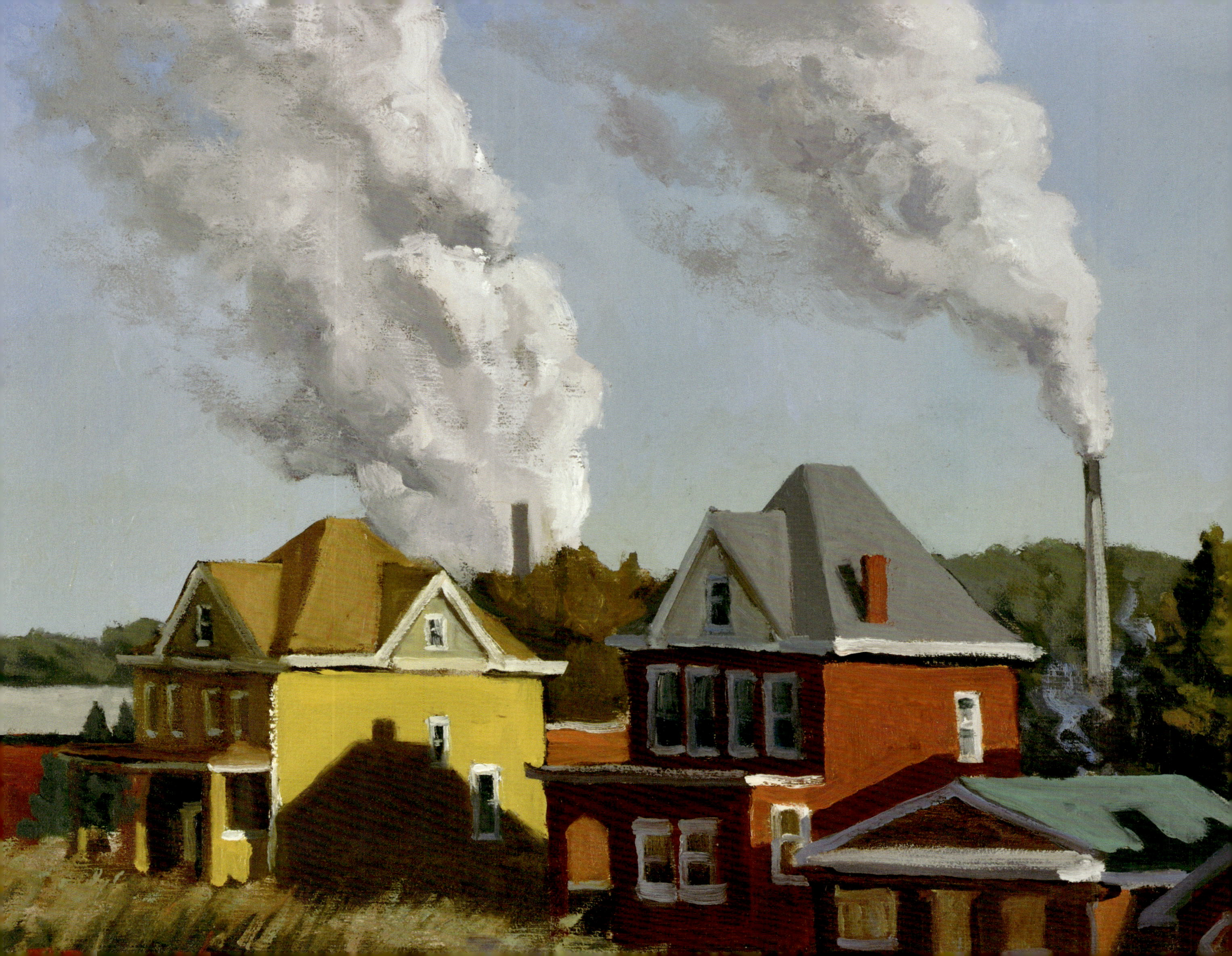

CONTENTS

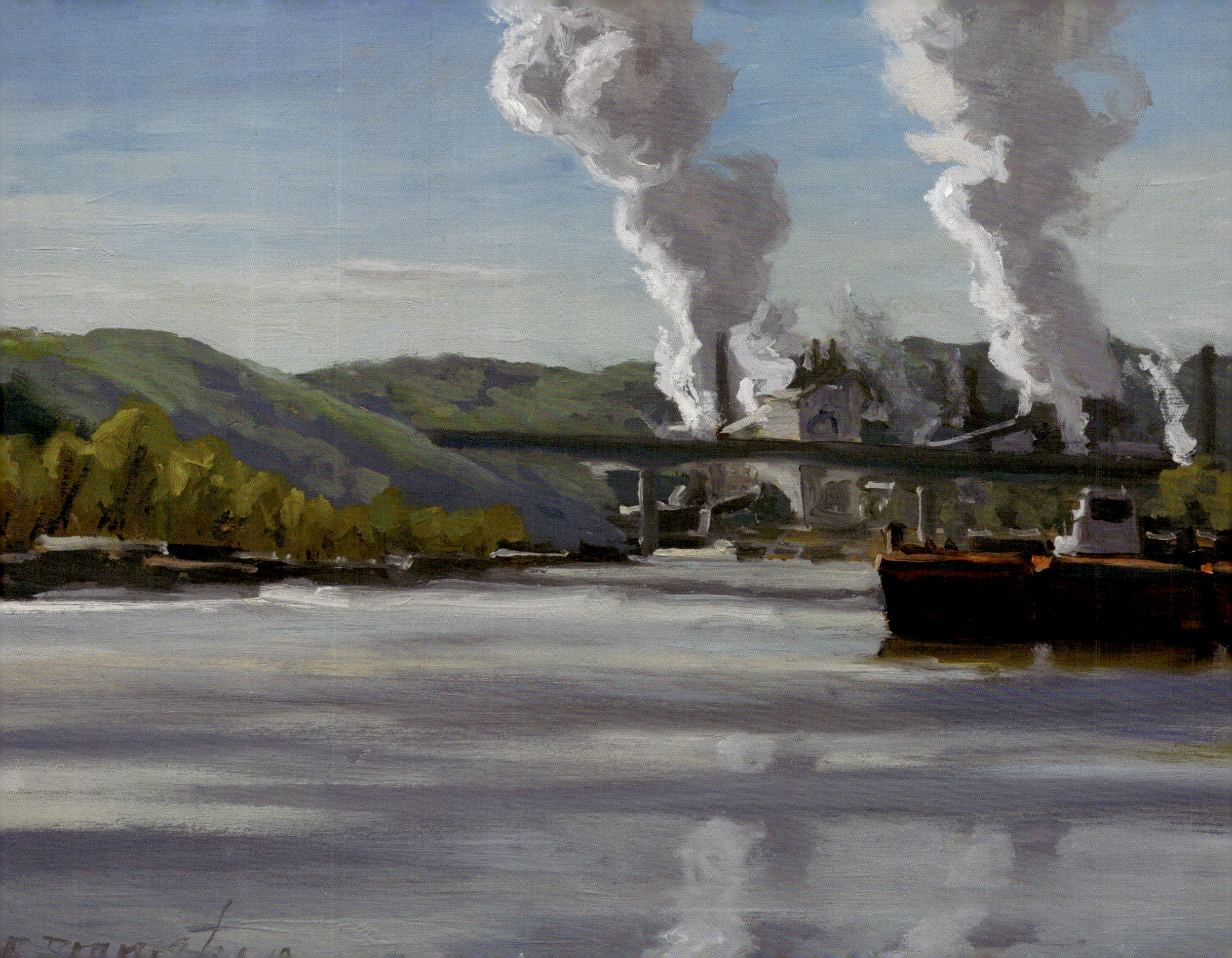

FOREWORD

THE MONONGAHELA RIVER STRETCHES 130 MILES FROM north-central West Virginia, up the Allegheny Plateau, to Pittsburgh, Pennsylvania. The so-called Mon Valley, as much a state of mind as a piece of geography, includes dozens of towns and cities along the river in western Pennsylvania—communities like Brownsville, Belle Vernon, Charleroi, Monessen, Donora, Elizabeth, Clairton, McKeesport, Duquesne, and Braddock. This was part of the greatest manufacturing base in the world from the late nineteenth century until World War II: a monumental machine of innovation, creativity, and resilience—a network of rugged, brawny manufactories along both the Monongahela River and, beyond Pittsburgh, the Ohio River, into which the Mon flows.

The state of mind of the Mon Valley has always been one characterized by the cherishing of hard physical work and intense community pride. During the Pittsburgh region's great industrial era, the Mon Valley was the heart of enterprise, for the region and the nation. The people of these cities and towns were renowned for their commitment to hard, challenging work in the steel plants, metalworking mills, glass works, coal mines, and coke works that lined the river.

The name of the river derives from a Native American word that translates, roughly, as "falling banks." It refers to the unstable terrain in the shale and coal-rich Mon Valley. The river often runs a dark brown when heavy rains fall along its length. And it became one of the most polluted rivers in America because of the very industries that provided income and inspiration for working men and women as well as owners and managers.

Today, the Mon Valley's vaunted industrial might is a thing of the past. During the 1970s, 1980s, and 1990s, as heavy industry beat a relentless retreat from western Pennsylvania, the valley lost most of its mills and manufactories. Globalization and changes in technology cost the region dearly, but no area paid a heavier price than the valley.

Unemployment became rampant, crime and drugs invaded, and so many of the beautiful old towns and cities in the valley were vastly diminished by economic decline and abandonment. A review of the town and city centers along the river paints a discouraging picture of attractive old buildings that have severely deteriorated. Not all of the valley has suffered, but much of it continues to struggle, even as nearby Pittsburgh has enjoyed a cultural and economic renaissance.

It is the ideal time for an artistic sensibility like Ron Donoughe's to come to study, understand and paint the scenes of this still fascinating and often beautiful region. Donoughe has spent decades painting the various neighborhoods of Pittsburgh and its nearby environs. In addition, he has often studied and painted the hills and valleys and farms around his hometown of Loretto, Pennsylvania, as well as the mills in the "Scalp Level" region of Johnstown famous for a school of devoted plein air painters who made the beauty of the region well known.

Donoughe, who has spent thirty years around Pittsburgh fulfilling the advice offered by a college art instructor—"paint what you know"—has taken his skill and his plein air artist's eye to the Mon Valley for the past year to create a new project: *Brownsville to Braddock: Paintings and Observations of the Monongahela River Valley*. In so doing, he has managed to capture both the sadness of the valley's decline and the inherent strength and beauty of its history, its architecture, and its people. It is likely that this exhibit will help rekindle some of the great spirit here that has always been at the heart of the pride of the tough people who inhabit these towns and cities.

In fact, one of the wonders captured in Donoughe's research and his work is that the proud spirit of the region lives strong today. Although economic hardship has changed the landscape for most people in the valley, they still take deep pride in their traditions: in addition to a commitment to hard work, these include a direct, honest way of doing business, the kind of neighborliness that shows itself in caring for and helping each other, and an abiding sense of community and loyalty to the region.

Donoughe himself grew up near Loretto, in Cambria County, a community similar in many ways to the environs of the Mon Valley. He trained at Indiana University of Pennsylvania and has made a career as one of the most successful painters in the Pittsburgh region. Most recently, his *90 Pittsburgh Neighborhoods* exhibit, which came out of a dedication to capturing the feel of the city's numerous subcommunities, is a beautiful evocation of the beauty, the architecture, the streets and skies, and the feeling of the city itself. The exhibit is now a part of the collection at the Senator John Heinz History Center in Pittsburgh, and is on permanent display there.

The qualities that make Donoughe so exceptional in creating the feel of a region can be found in the words of Barbara L. Jones, curator at the Westmoreland Museum of American Art in Greensburg: "Ron captures not only the essence of a subject or place, but a moment in time as well . . . Ron is drawn intuitively to the sites that he paints by color, light, atmosphere, texture, shadow, shape, and form. . . . He paints in all seasons and at all times of the day in an effort to translate particular places and moments into art."[1]

Ron Donoughe has become one of the region's most popular painters, as well as one of the most prolific. His works reside in many personal art collections in homes throughout the region, as well as at institutions like the Westmoreland, the Duquesne Club, the Southern Alleghenies Museum of Art, the University Museum at Indiana University of Pennsylvania, Westminster College, the Children's Museum of Pittsburgh, the Senator John Heinz History Center, and others.

Eventually the Mon Valley—like Pittsburgh to the north—will emerge from its economic doldrums and prosper again; a prosperity that will quite likely be built on the rich heritage of architecture and history that distinguishes the region. Meanwhile, it is of great value to the region, and to the world at large, that Donoughe has found the skill to capture the Mon Valley at this time in its journey.

— MAXWELL KING

Past president of the Heinz Endowments and the Pittsburgh Foundation, former editor of *Philadelphia Inquirer*, and the author of *The Good Neighbor: The Life and Work of Fred Rogers*.

---

1. Ron Donoughe, *Essence of Pittsburgh: The Paintings of Ron Donoughe in the Plein Air Style* (Pittsburgh: Pittsburgh Filmmakers/Pittsburgh Center for the Arts, 2006), 8.

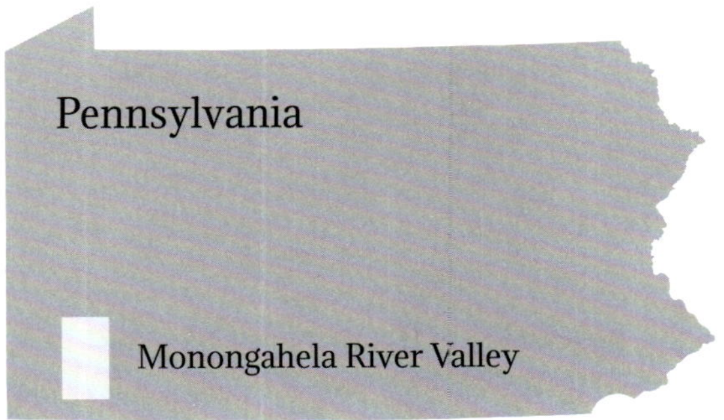

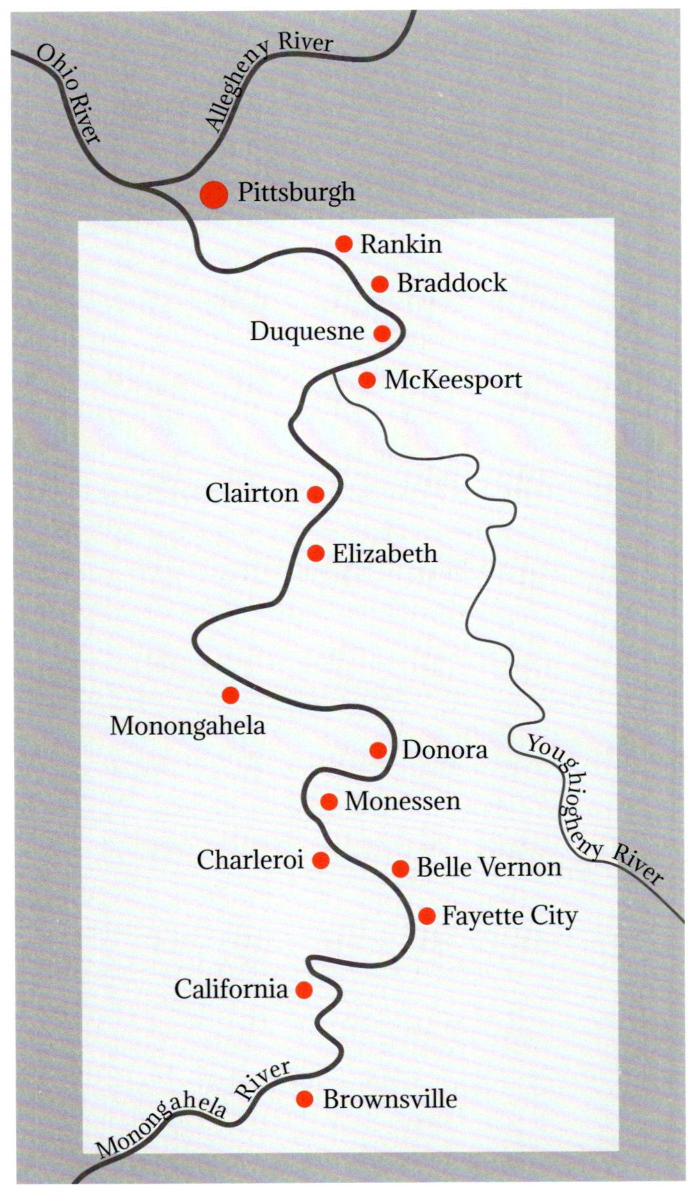

MON VALLEY MAP

The significant history of Brownsville dates back to Native Americans. I decided to make Brownsville the southernmost point of my project because of its significant industrial past.

INTRODUCTION

FOR THE LAST THIRTY YEARS I'VE BEEN DOCUMENTING WESTERN
Pennsylvania through paintings. Many of my projects have been multipanel installations of plein air paintings. Visiting a region over a twelve-month period is my way of learning about a particular place. In addition to painting the ninety neighborhoods of Pittsburgh, I've explored Indiana, Lawrence, Cambria, and Blair Counties, making similar projects. Because I prefer to paint on location, it makes sense for me to spend a significant amount of time getting to know the area and the people who live there.

The Monongahela River Valley has a lot in common with my own roots in Cambria County. Both have bucolic landscapes and a contrasting industrial aesthetic. The rivers that run through Johnstown were once lined with railroads, belching coke ovens, and steelmaking facilities. Most of that is gone now, too, leaving behind a city that has struggled. It's for these reasons that the Monongahela Valley river towns have such a familiarity to me. It's almost like I've gone home.

Over twelve months I painted more than fifty pieces from Brownsville to Braddock. I approached this subject as a way to document a region with a rich history, and perhaps shine a light on it with my brushes and paints. Before this project, I personally knew very little about the region and now believe the Mon Valley is often overlooked. I hope that changes.

All of the paintings for this project, I should note, were completed before the COVID-19 pandemic occurred. I was fortunate because I often met people along the way who offered personal stories of joy and sorrows. People are typically curious to see an artist in their neighborhood, which is an interesting way for me to make a connection with total strangers. And in a larger sense, I see these paintings as a conversation with a region, an opportunity for a dialogue and an invitation to explore. My painting process intertwines art, regional history, and life.

The stretch of approximately forty miles along the Monongahela River offers a fascinating history that really tells the success story of western Pennsylvania. I chose Brownsville as the southernmost town to start in and ended with Braddock, following the directional flow of the river north. First settled in 1785, Brownsville served as a trading post and gateway to pioneers heading west. Many industries such as riverboat building, glassmaking, and coke and iron production helped to make it an important town, as did easy access to Pittsburgh and onward via the Ohio River.

Braddock seemed like the proper place to end. The sprawling Mon Valley Works–Edgar Thomson Plant is a throwback to the industrial revolution. It's been in operation since Andrew Carnegie built it in 1872. I've painted it many times over the years from several vistas, and remain fascinated by its industrial beauty.

Because I'm a landscape painter, people generally do not appear in my work. Painting the places people inhabit is my way of capturing the human condition. The photo portraits here were taken six months after I finished the paintings. The individuals featured, whose ages ranged from thirteen to ninety-six, were mostly selected from areas where I had made paintings. They provided personalized voices from the Mon Valley and help tell its current story.

After painting the region for an entire year, I could not help but be surprised by how much natural beauty is there. And although economic hardship is visually obvious, a confident and hopeful spirit remains intact.

— RON DONOUGHE

BROWNSVILLE TO BRADDOCK

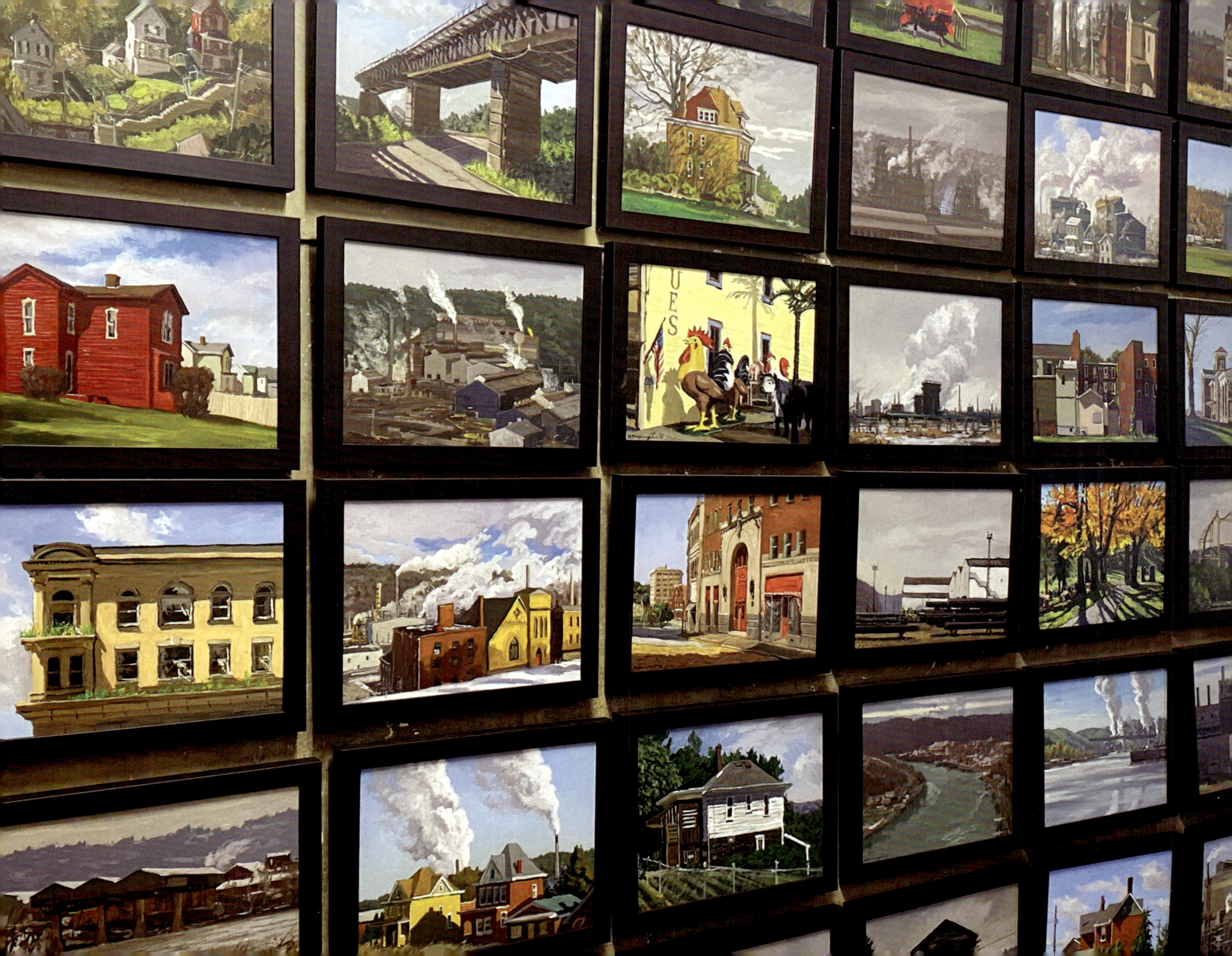

PAINTINGS AND VOICES OF
THE MON RIVER VALLEY

BOWMAN'S CASTLE

Brownsville

Also known as Nemacolin Castle, this architectural gem was being renovated while I painted it.

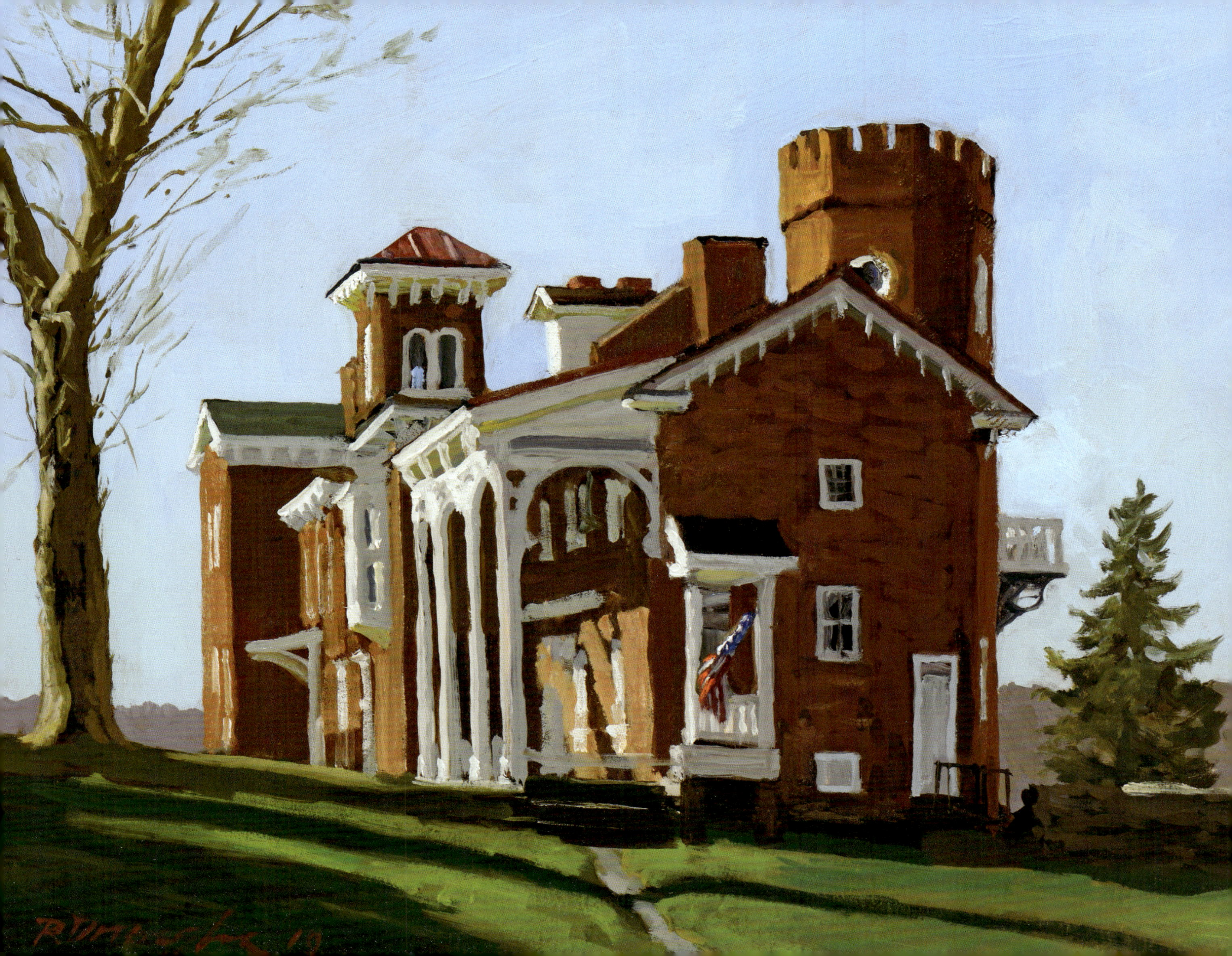

LANE BANE BRIDGE

West Brownsville

This bridge spans the Monongahela River at Brownsville. It was interesting to experience it at the edge of the water, especially while barges gracefully pushed ripples toward my easel.

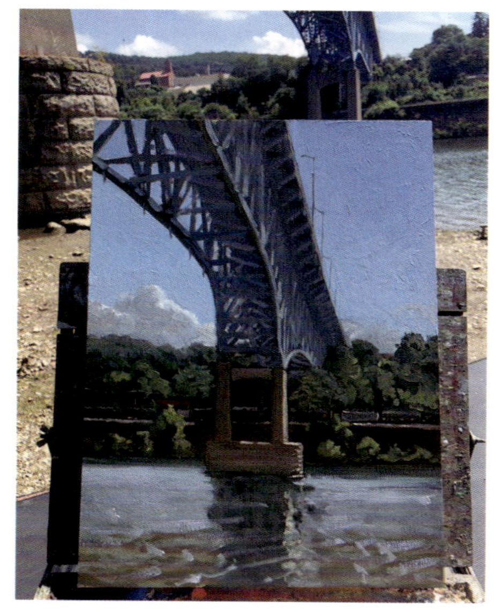

Painting on location comes with many challenges. I'm often asked why I don't just paint from photos. Well, sometimes I do. But there is something special that happens when you stand and look closely at the subject for two hours. I call it the Zen of seeing. The spirit of place becomes part of the experience and influences the painting.

For the perspective of this painting— sometimes referred to as a "worm's-eye view"— I wanted to convey the extreme height of this structure and how it felt from where I stood.

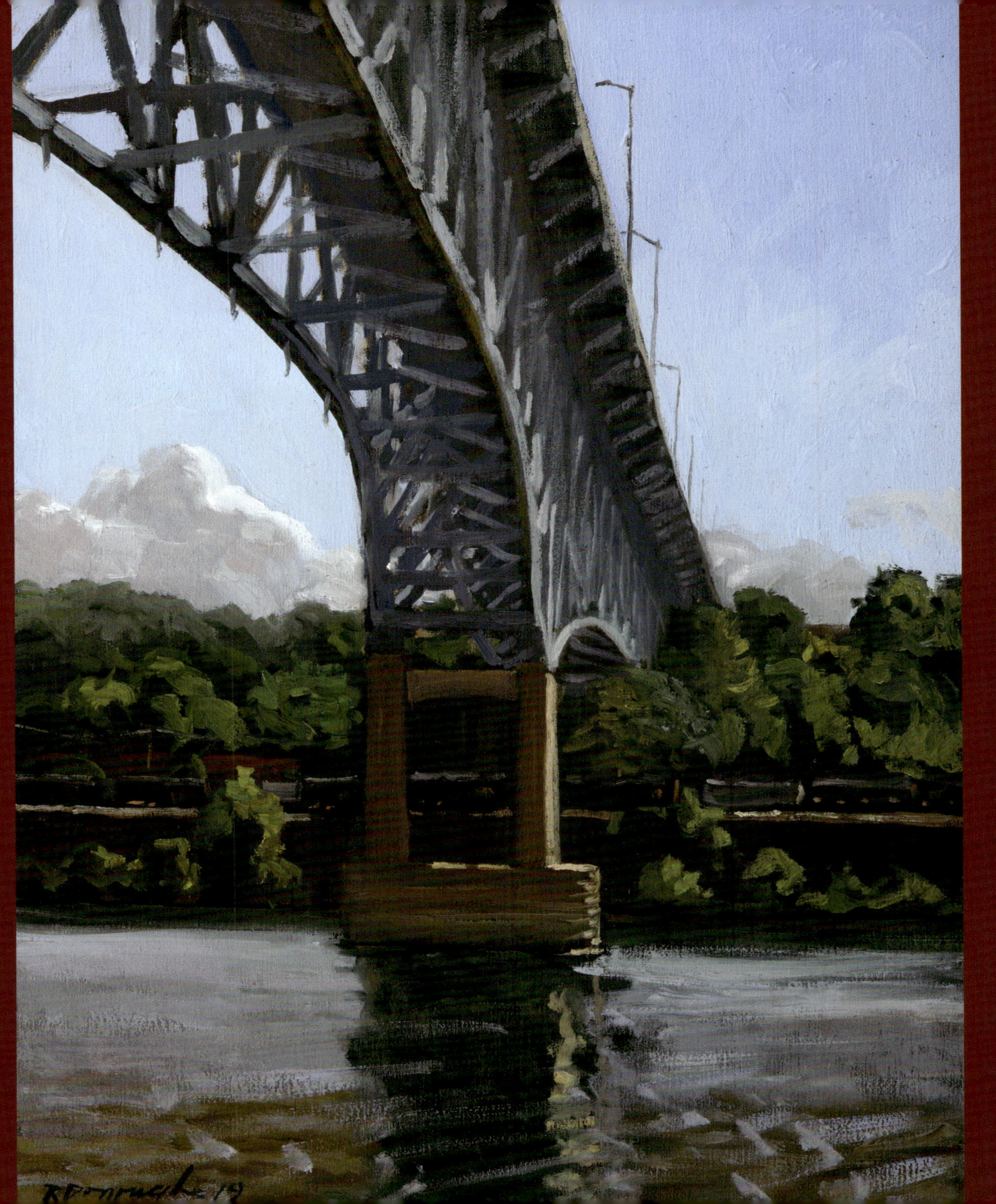

ALL ABOARD

Trains are inexplicitly interesting, especially a red one that contrasts with a green background. This one sits at the edge of California University of Pennsylvania campus, next to the town library. I was inspired by the industrial design and the careful attention to detail.

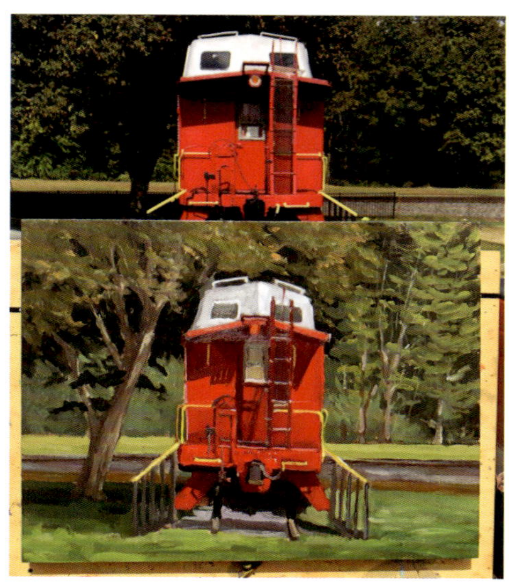

The photographer for Cal U showed up to take a few shots of me for their magazine while working on location.

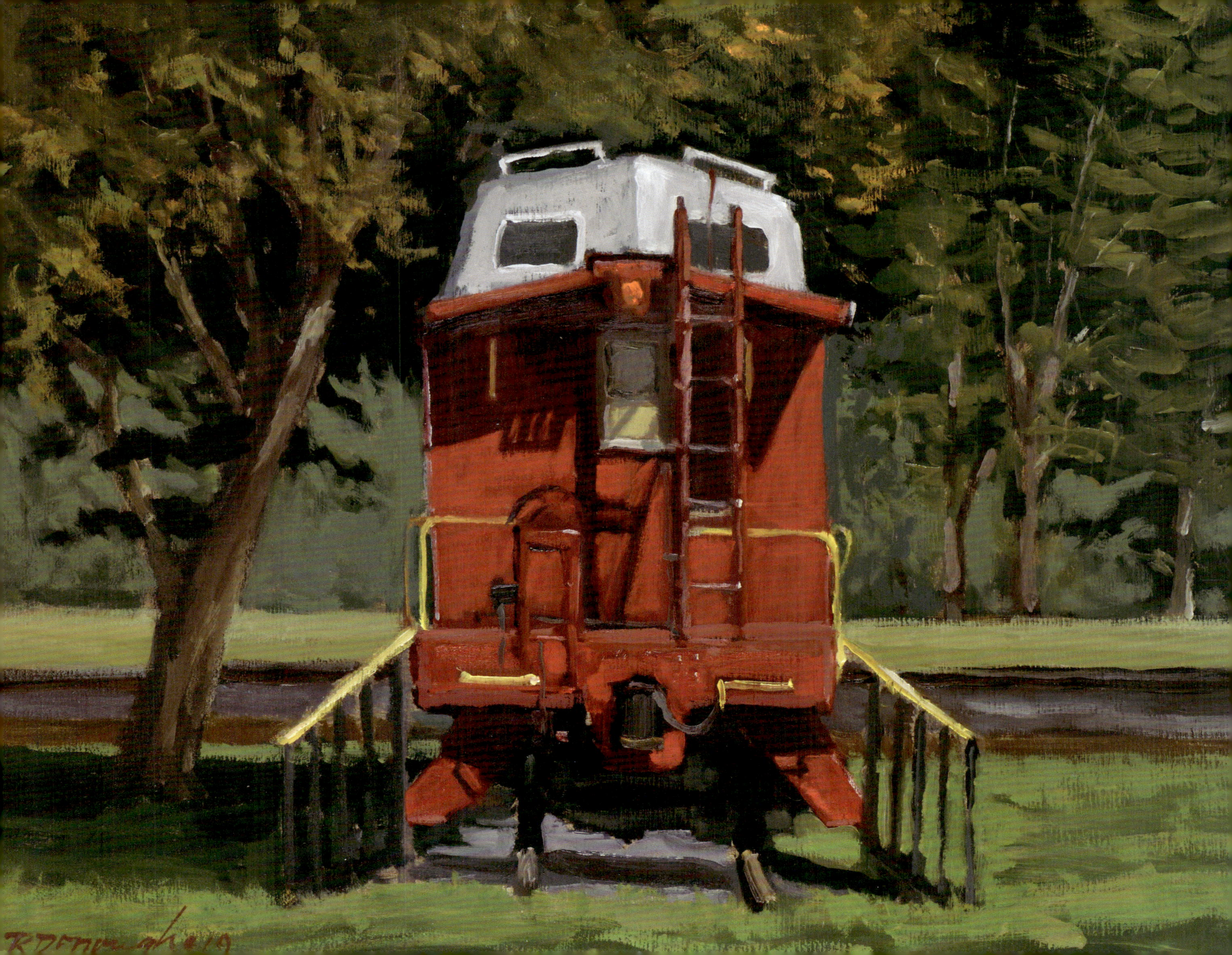

UNION STATION

Many large buildings in Brownsville are substantial and well designed. Hopefully they'll be rescued before they collapse into themselves. The history of the town as the gateway to Pittsburgh and the West makes it an important part of the region's heritage.

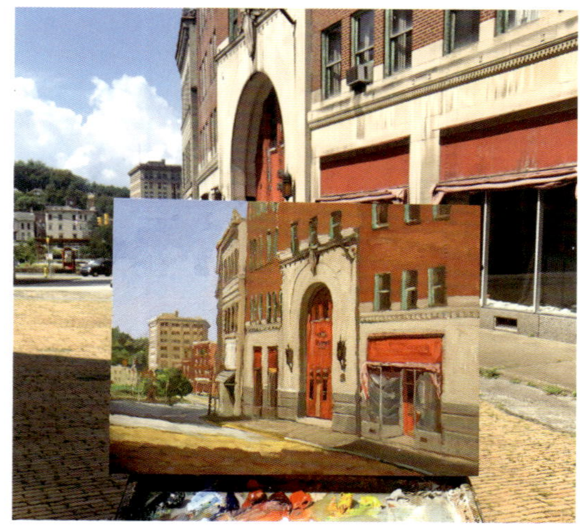

The early morning shadows moved quickly. My initial plan was to have Union Station partly covered in shade cast from a neighboring structure, but I settled for a shadowed foreground.

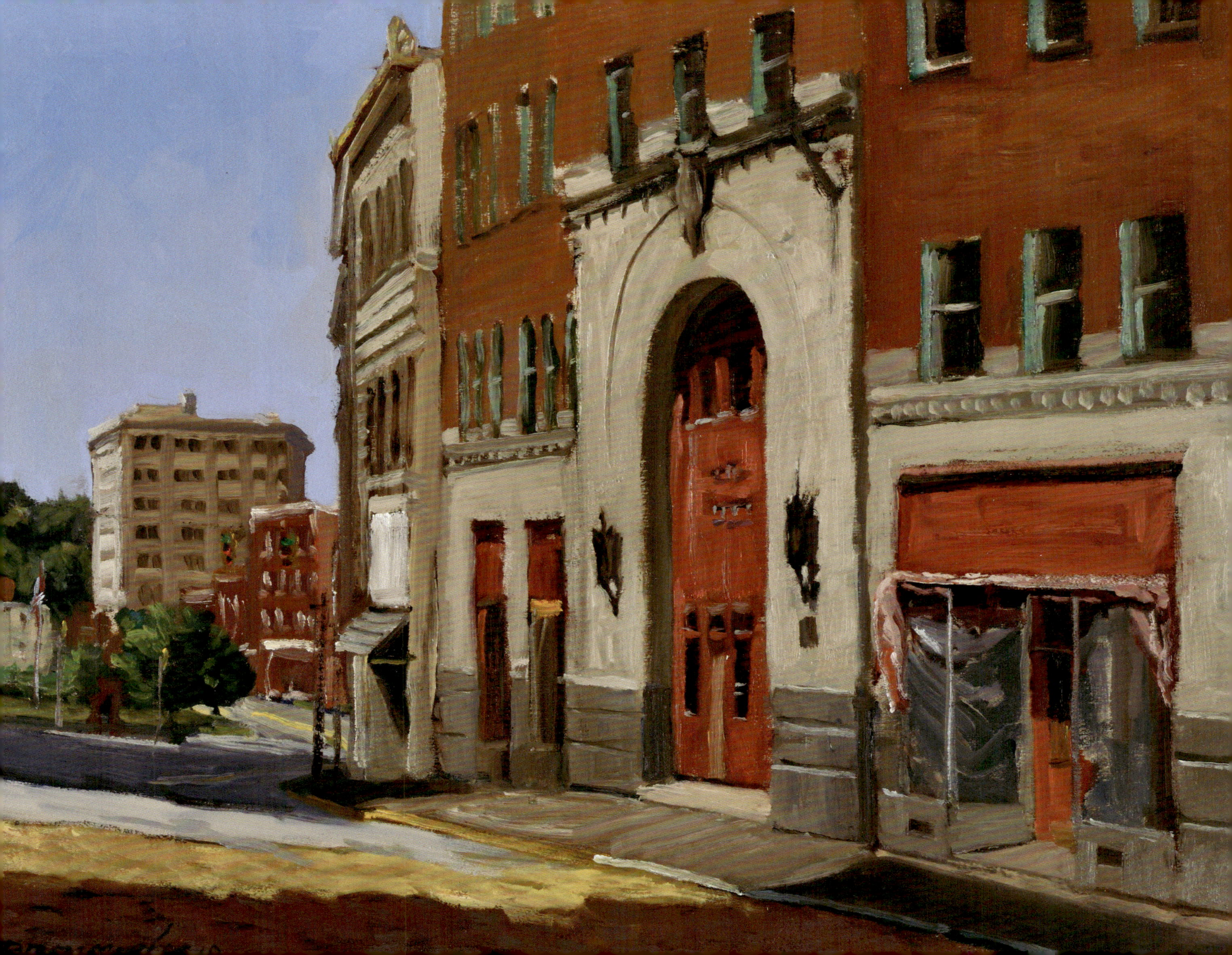

VISTA CAL. U

California

After visiting California University of Pennsylvania, I found this vista on a perch that overlooked the Monongahela River, the town, and the university. The April day was misting, which enveloped the landscape with a soft light.

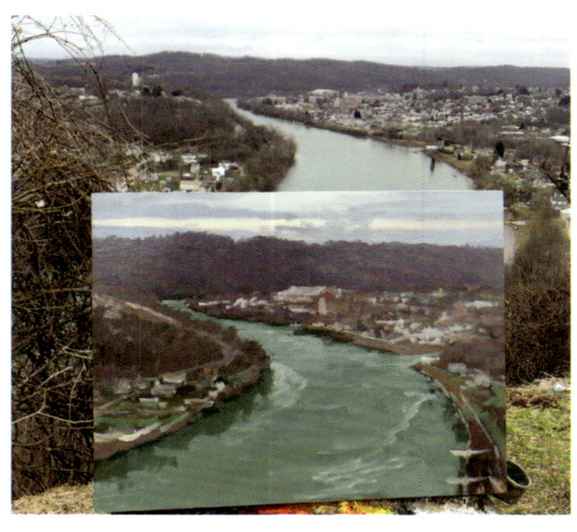

I'm often trying to describe what happens in the atmosphere, between the subject and myself. It's important to understand the atmospheric effects in order to mix the proper colors.

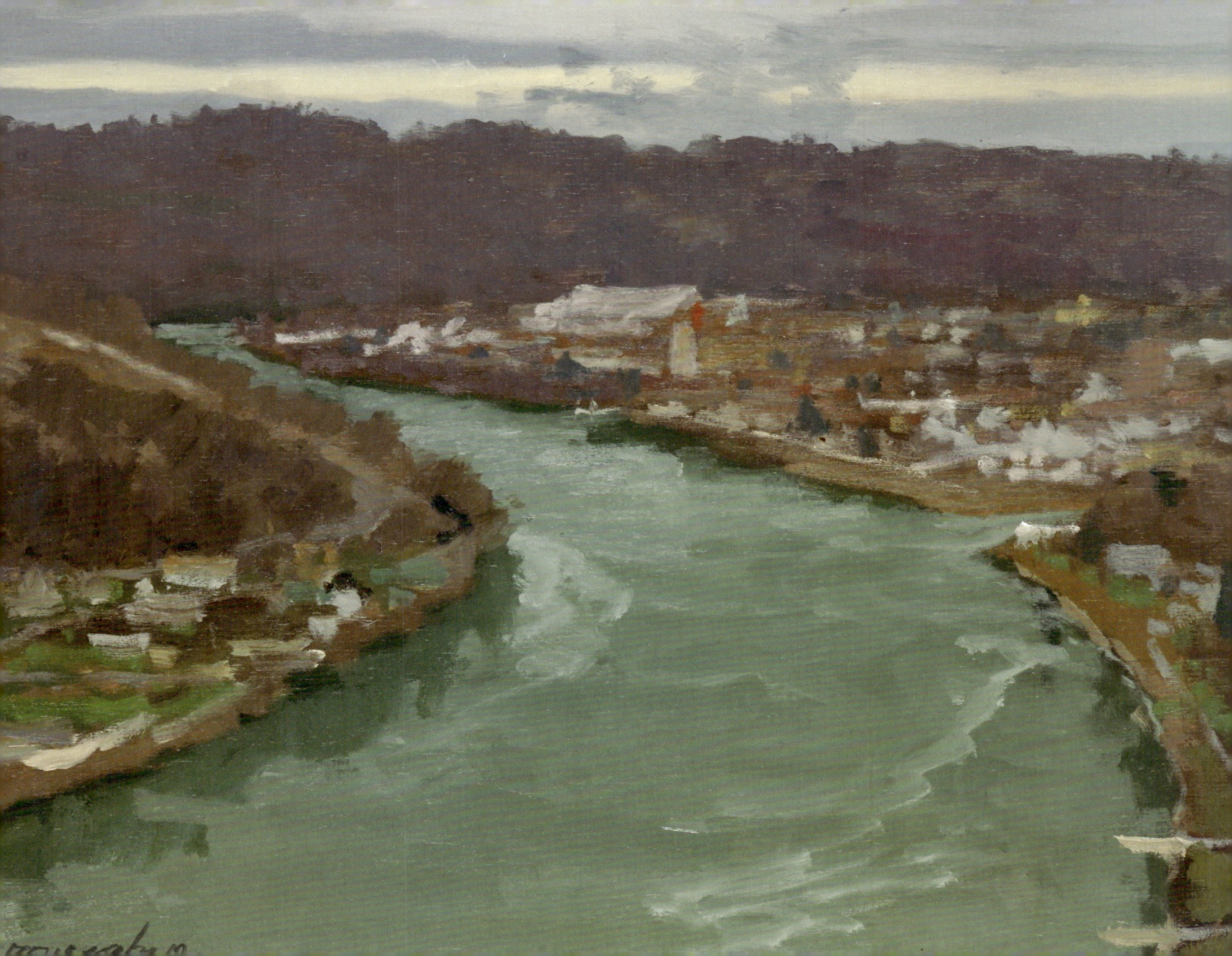

WATER STREET

Belle Vernon

This painting was completed as I stood under a railroad bridge. My intent was to paint the distant bridge and marina. However, it occurred to me that the structures built to carry rail traffic were built with huge cut stones, covered in shades of black and gray. It's an interesting contrast next to the lapping bluish water.

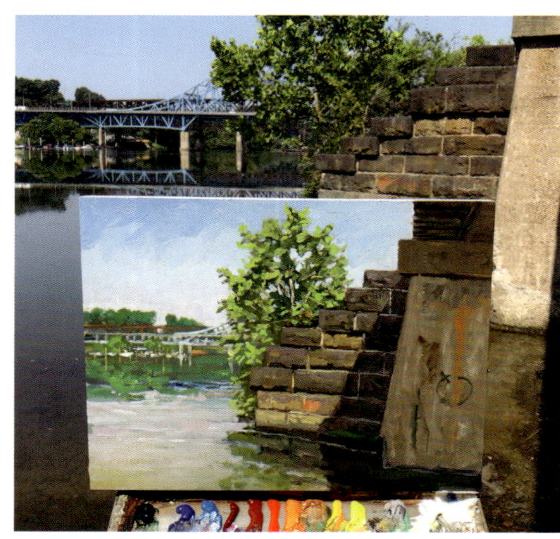

Locomotives pulling tons of bituminous coal rumbled overhead as I worked like a troll under a bridge. I could actually feel the ground shake.

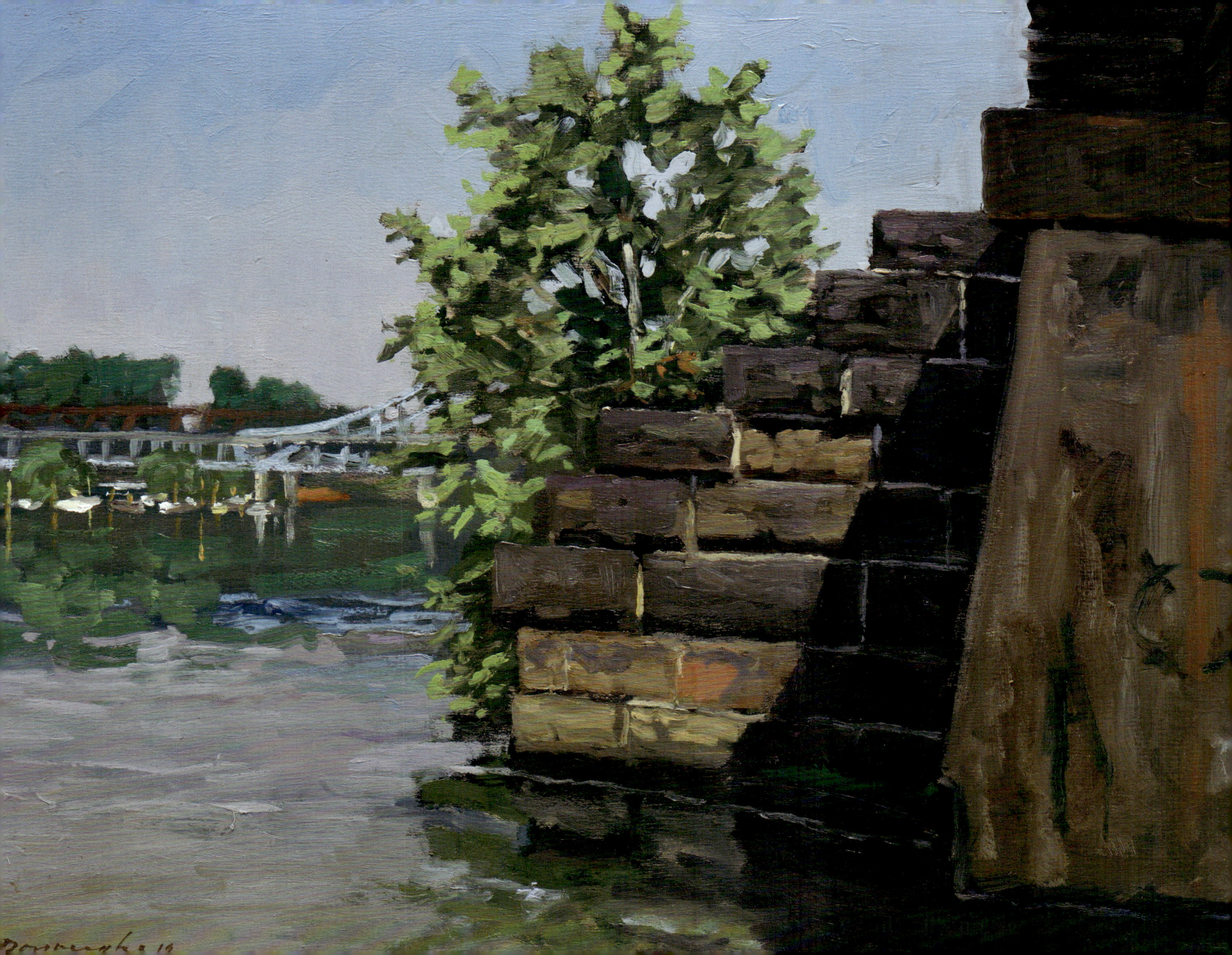

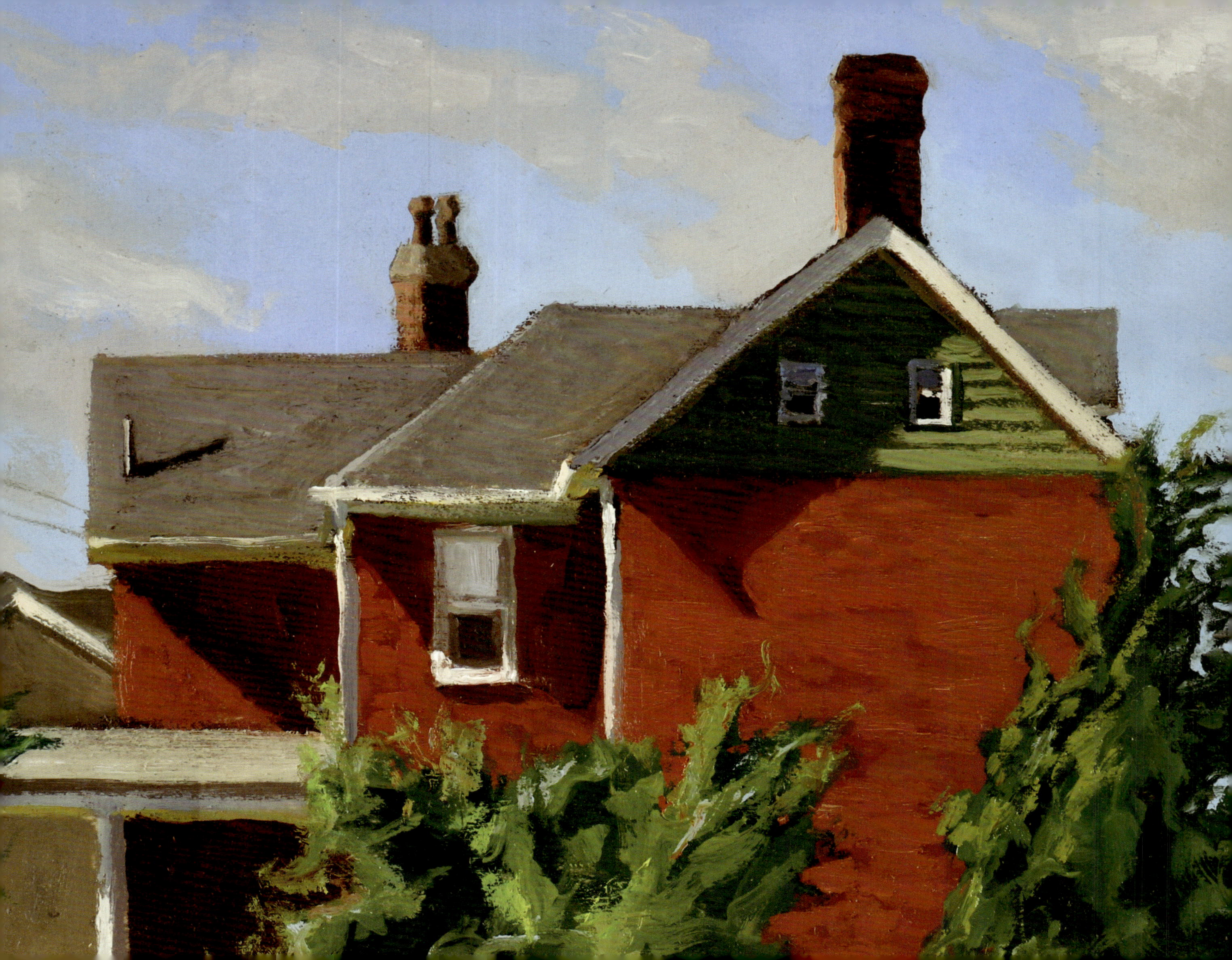

LISA

Lisa is happy to call Elizabeth Borough home and is excited about its future. She says a new brewery is taking shape and her daughter recently opened a successful hair salon in town. Lisa would love to open a coffee shop next to her daughter's salon. Lisa is married to a former musician who is from Millvale and used to play in a popular band. "We've only ever had churches and a couple bars . . . we've got a beer brewery coming in right next to the candy shop. . . . Things are turning around. People are coming into the town. They're shopping. It's just wonderful. "

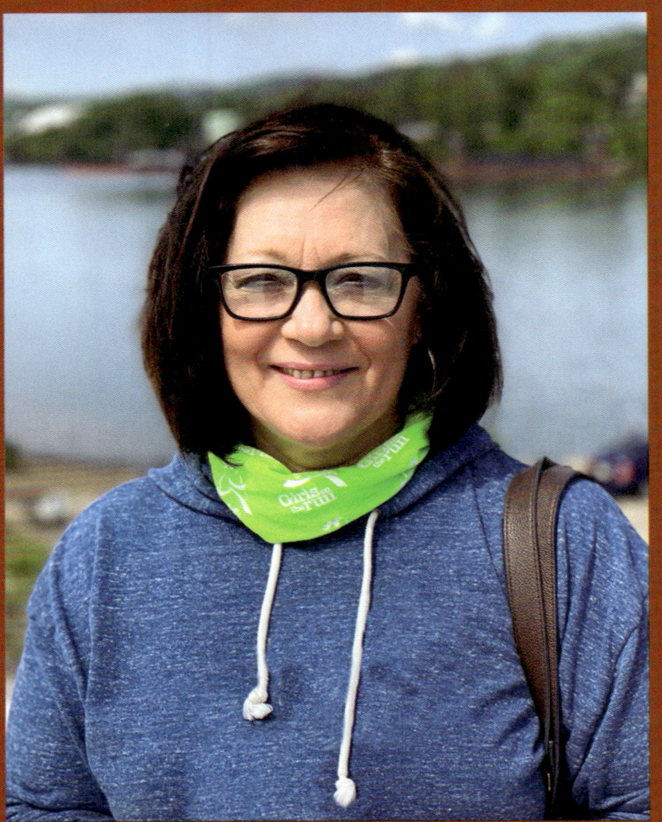

RED CLAPBOARD

North Charleroi

This red wood-sided house really stood out. Many houses in the valley were sided with brick or Inselbric (sometimes spelled Insulbrick). Those materials were popular in the region because they did not need to be painted—a big advantage considering the emissions from the nearby industries.

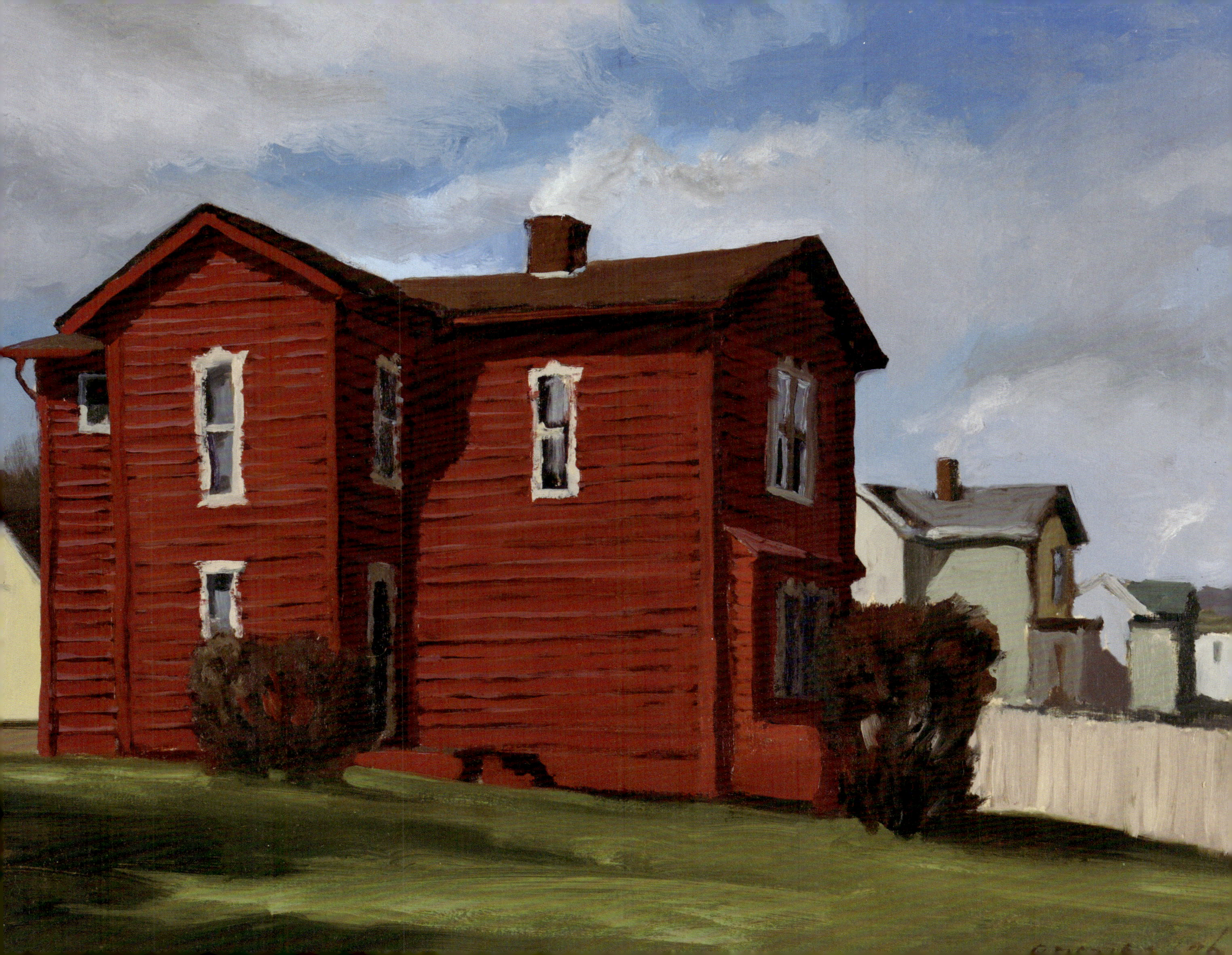

ROOSTER

Charleroi

Antique shops add a festive touch to many towns. These oversized farmyard creatures appeared to be leading a parade. I imagined them taking the flag and marching down McKean Avenue.

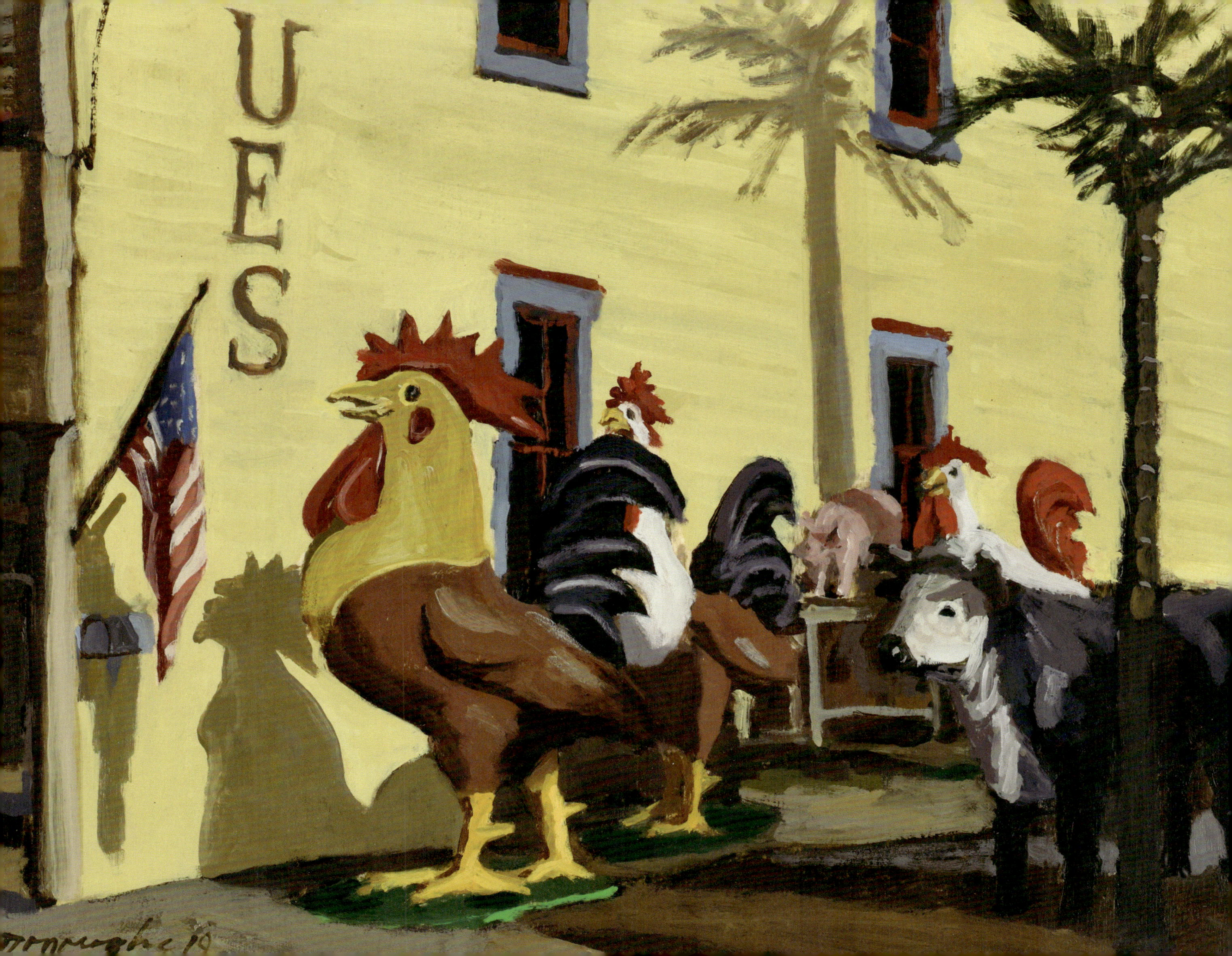
UES

A MEMORY

Monessen

A person close to me recalled her childhood memories at her grandparents' house in Monessen. Warm memories of this particular house inspired me to visit and also explore the river towns of the Monongahela River Valley. The people I've met shared many stories of family joy and sorrows. These oral histories add to the artistic experience, and in some way, make paintings more authentic.

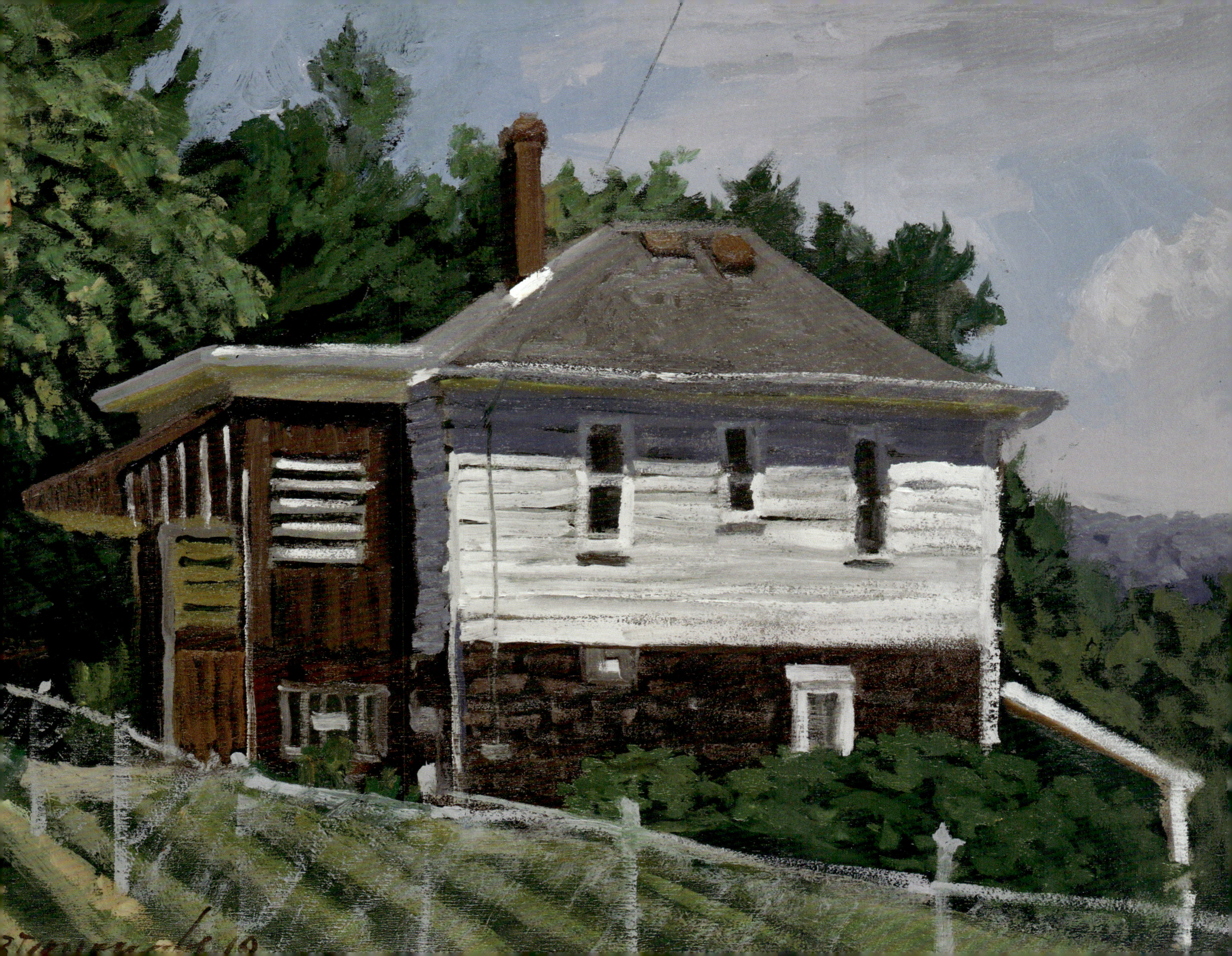

A SHADOW OF ITSELF

Many stately and historic structures are in peril. This one, the former Monessen Savings and Trust Building, is a fine example. Even as weeds grow from ledges, it calls out to be restored to its former glory.

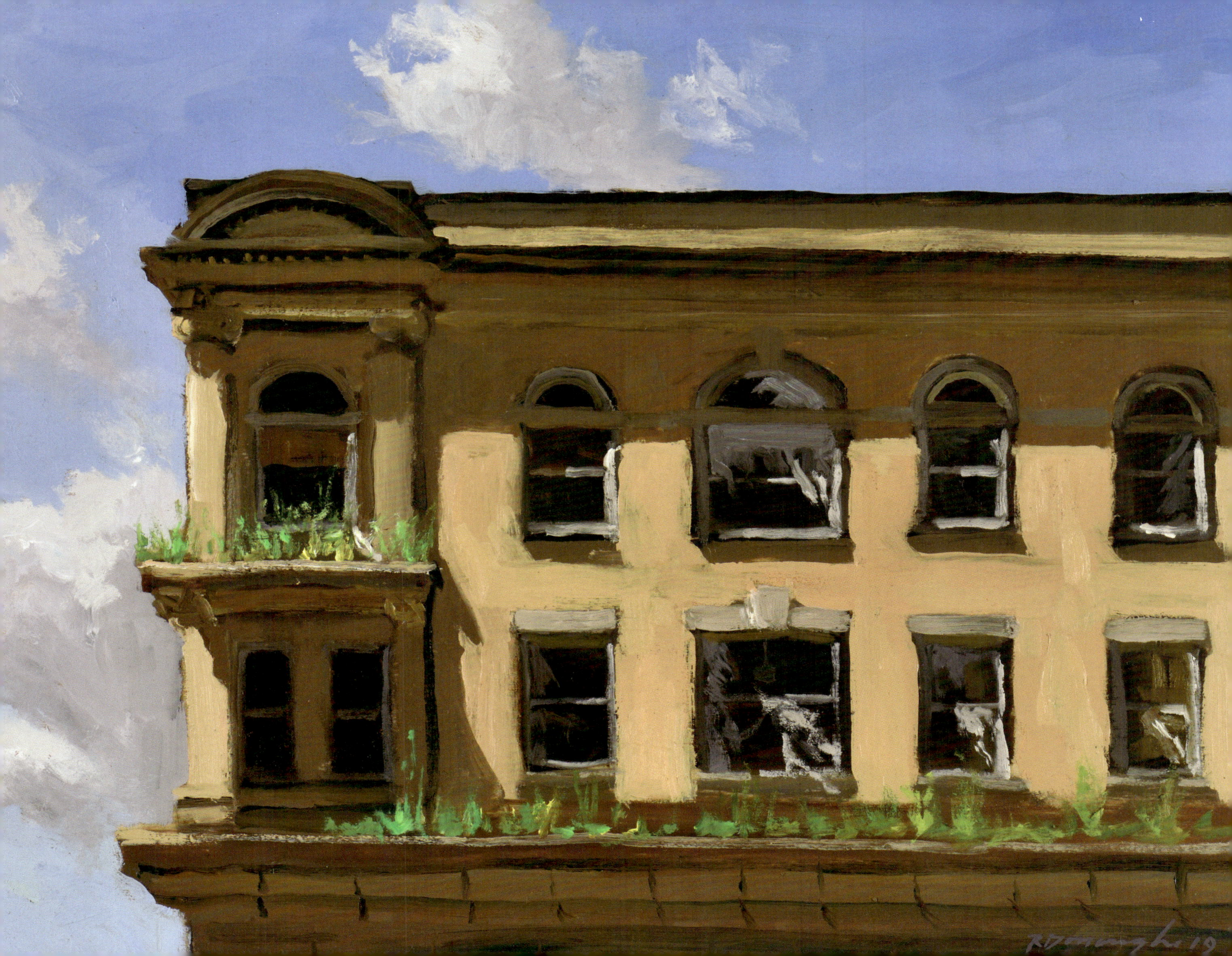

FIRE IN THE SKY

Where there is smoke, as well as fire and stacks, there must be an industrial facility. Apparently this eighty-year-old coke plant still has a future. These facilities were never designed to be aesthetic pieces of architecture, but I find them to be just that. They are living and breathing relics that remind me of the industrial past.

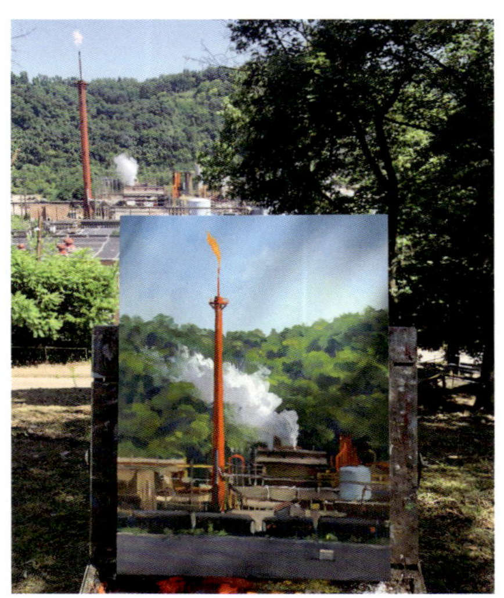

The local mailman stopped his van behind me, where he had an excellent view of my painting and the scene. He started telling me about the economic issues of the town and a short history of the mill I was painting.

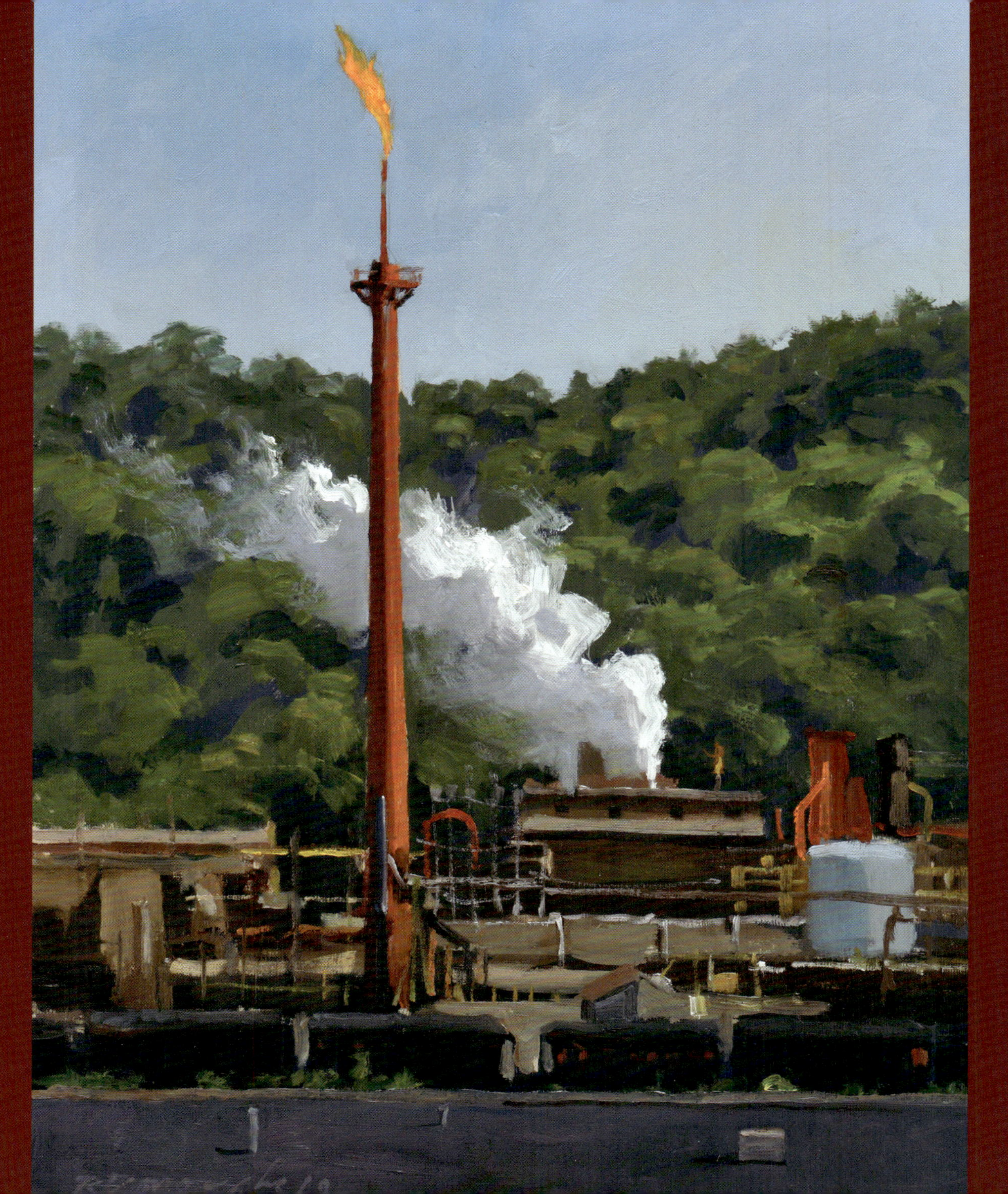

MONESSEN

Monessen

The steep hillside in Monessen allows for a wonderful vista of the town and its industry. This winter scene was quite cheerful as the skies cleared and the sun dappled the buildings.

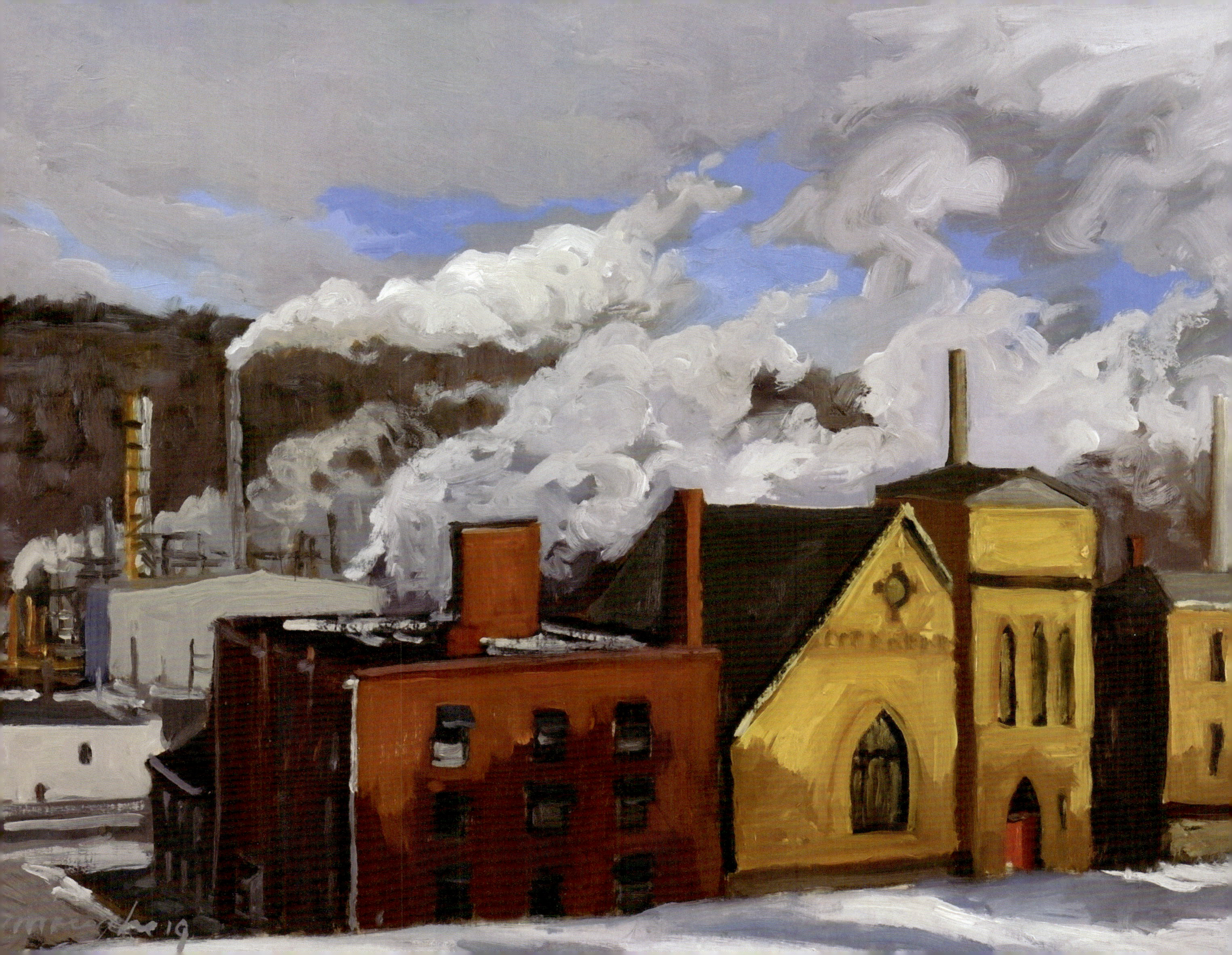

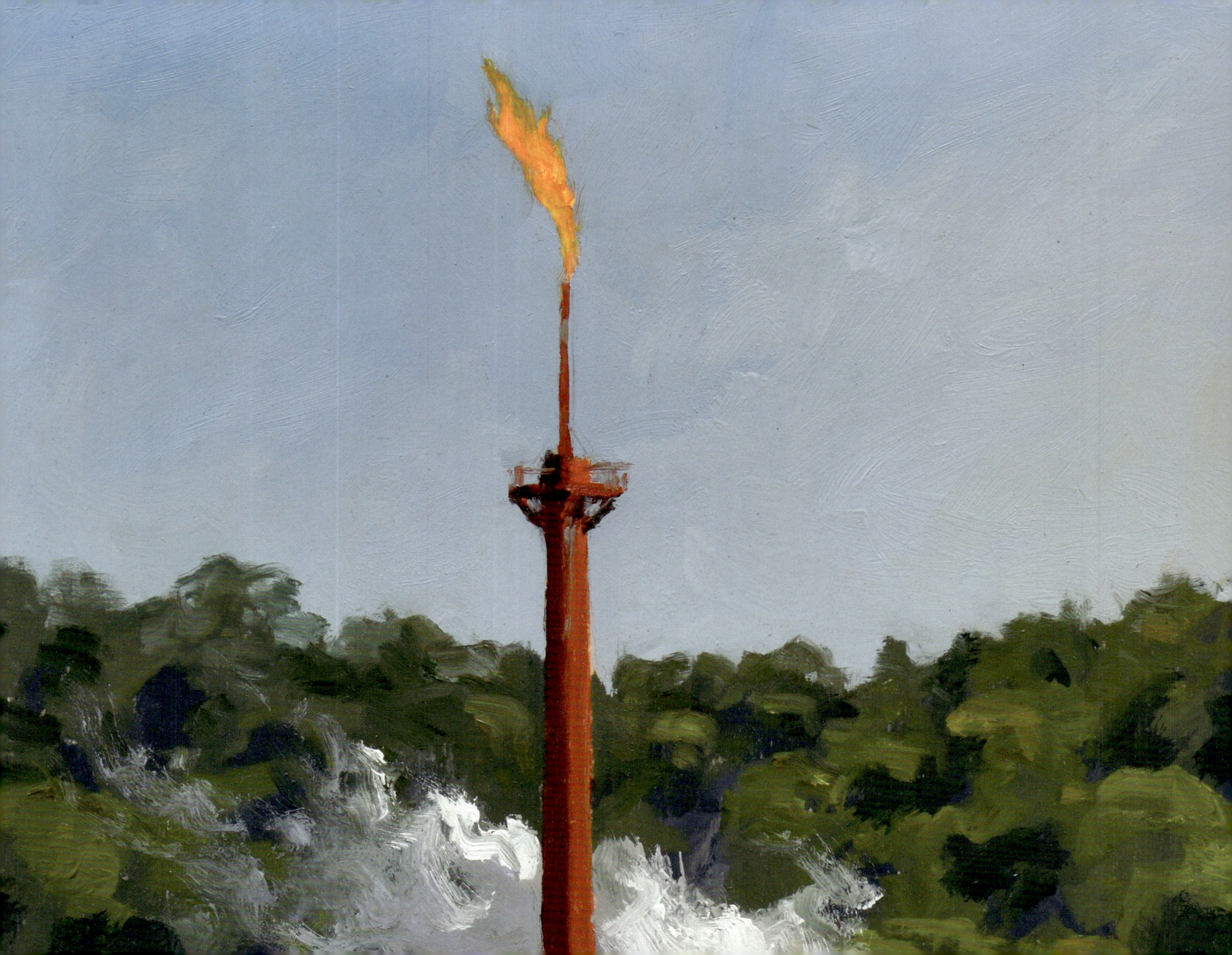

LOUISE

Louise is ninety-six years old and is retired after spending thirty-seven years as a public schoolteacher. Her late husband, who died in 1992, was also a teacher. The couple opened the Gondolier Restaurant in 1955 and ran it together for many years as well. She says their restaurant was the only pizza place in the Mon Valley. Things were thriving and they attracted customers from other towns like New Eagle, Charleroi, and Monongahela. After retirement, Louise continued tutoring students for thirty-five years. She was also the borough council president for many years and volunteers at the community food bank. She says we shouldn't get upset when the economy fluctuates because that's the nature of the economy. She says we just have to adjust and avoid complacency. "The pendulum swings. To me, the valley will always be a great valley. People will come and go, but it will be a great valley. The people make the valley."

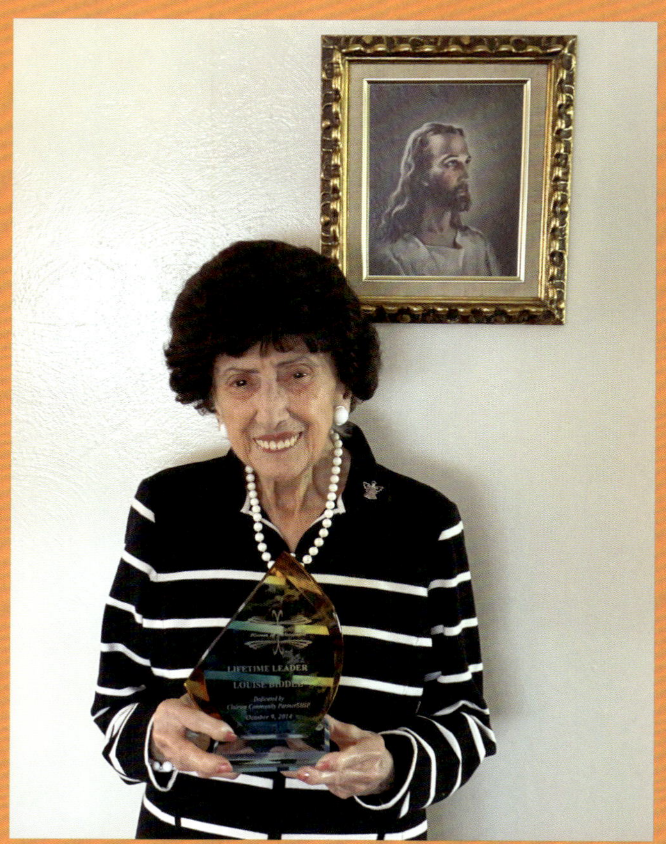

NOVEMBER LIGHT

Donora

Many of the river towns are laid out in a similar, but predictable format. The hillsides slope toward the river, where commerce occupies valuable real estate. The downtowns are situated closely, and then residential housing stretches up the steep hills. That's where the city steps play an important role. As I did this painting, I watched the daily ritual of "getting your steps in."

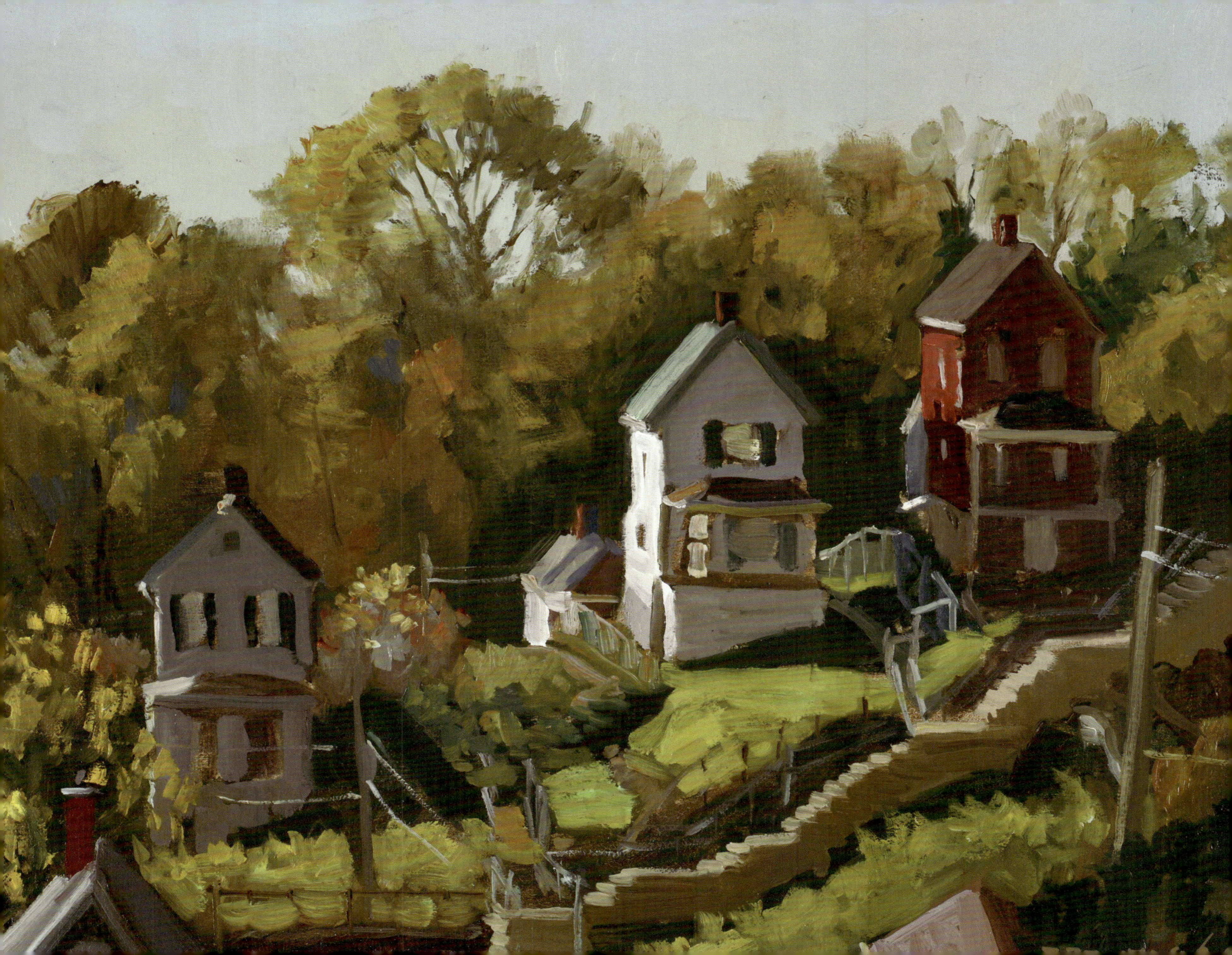

SAINT NICHOLAS ORTHODOX CHURCH

Donora

Churches are the most important structures of most neighborhoods. It is easy to understand why they were centers of immigrant faith. The architecture and craftsmanship speak to a dedicated community. This one is perched high on the hillside and enjoys a spectacular vista of Donora.

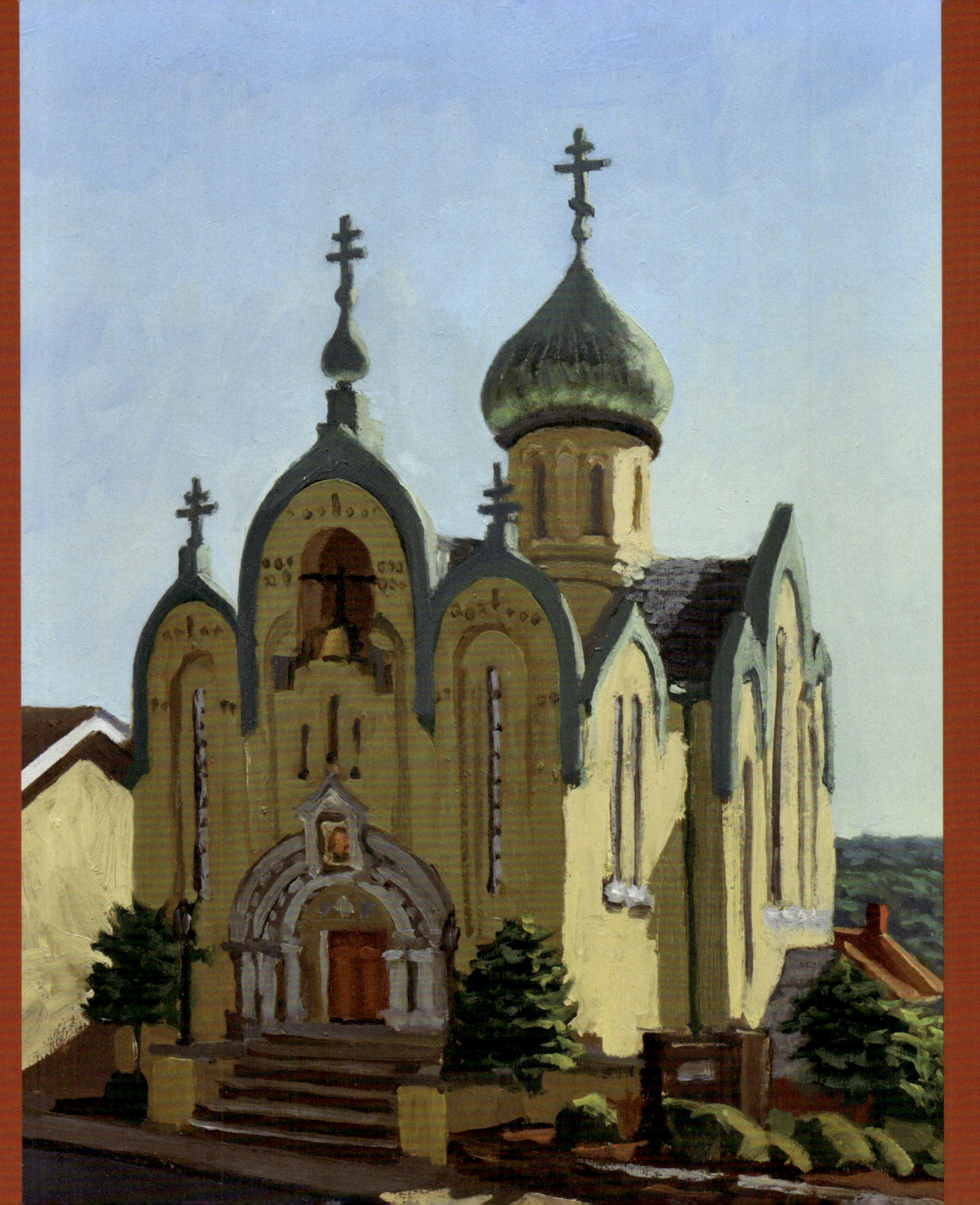

STORAGE TANK

Donora

Some things that are part of the landscape are easy to dismiss. Storage tanks fall into this category. Upon closer inspection, you realize they are actually quite beautiful in a simple, form-follows-function type of design.

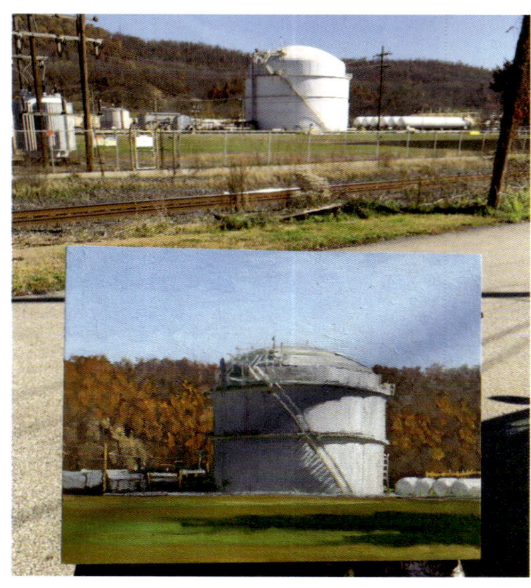

This was painted on a beautiful day in the valley. I had just seen a documentary about the Donora inversion of 1948, which killed and injured many residents. It was hard to imagine a point when the air pollution was so dense folks couldn't see across the street.

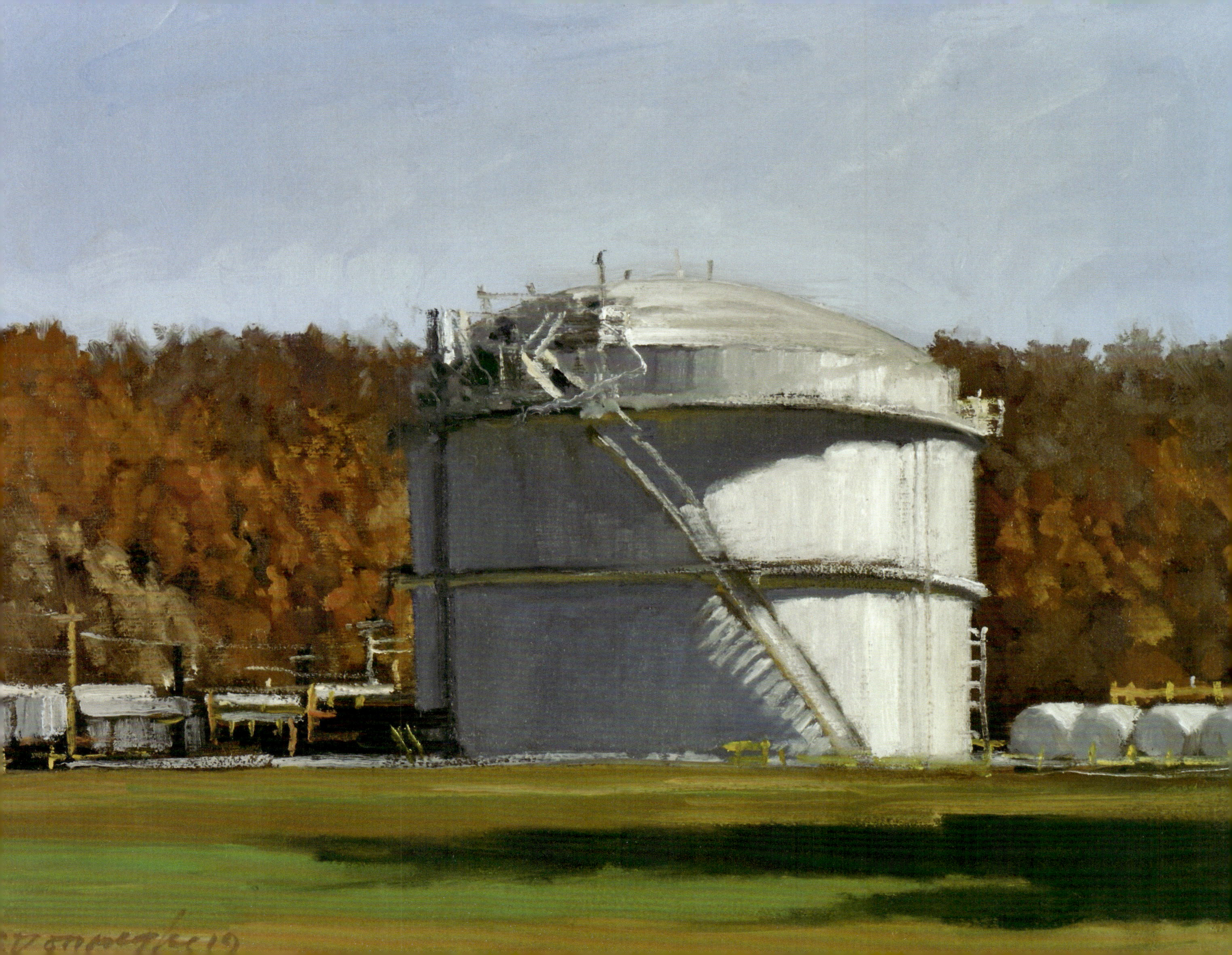

MONONGAHELA MANOR

Monongahela

This structure stands out because it's unlike the surrounding architecture. The residents are treated to an excellent view of the river.

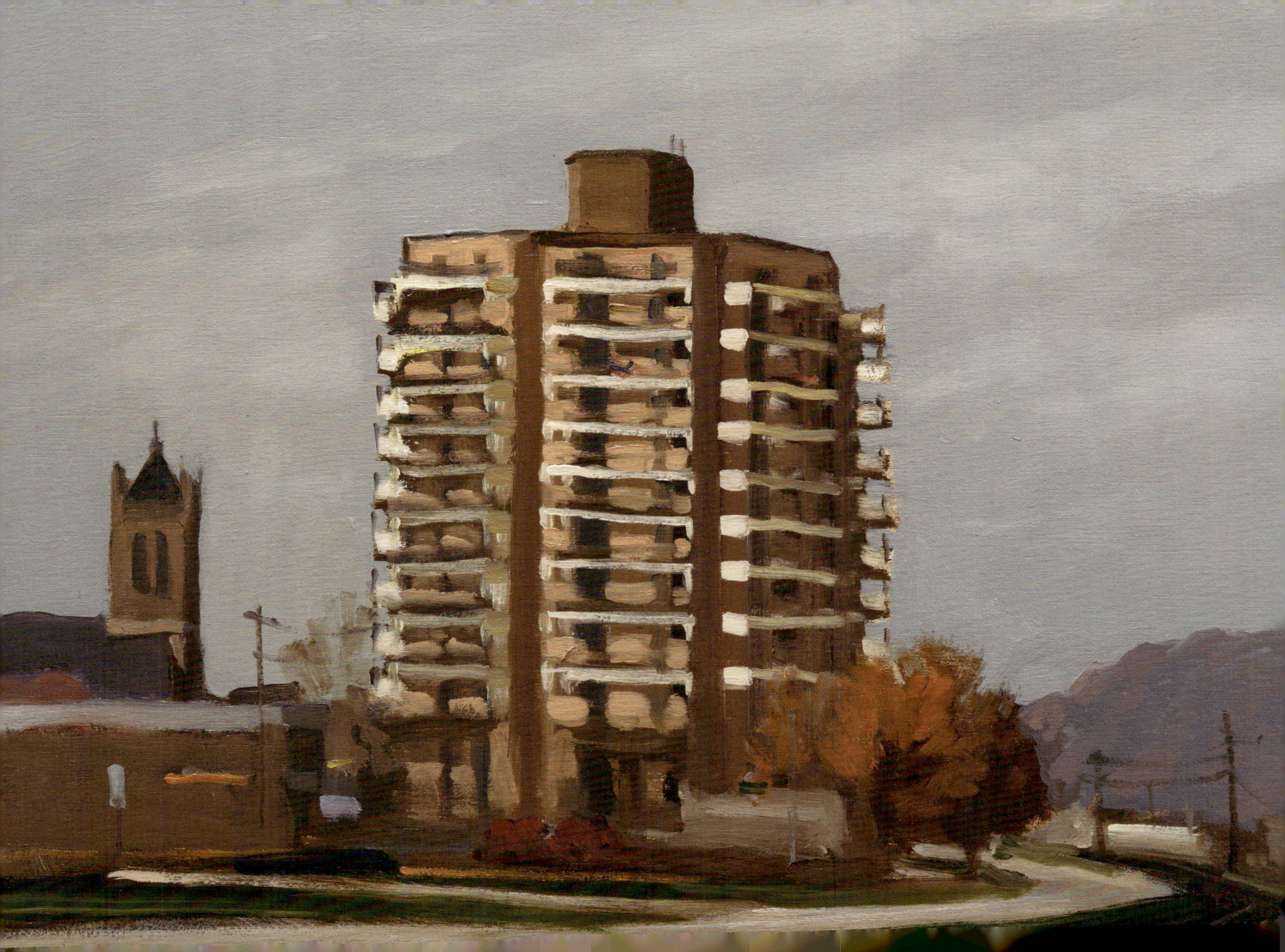

MONONGAHELA

Monongahela

The backs of buildings and alleyways have a geometry and texture that is quite different from the front. This was painted from the Monongahela Aquatorium Park.

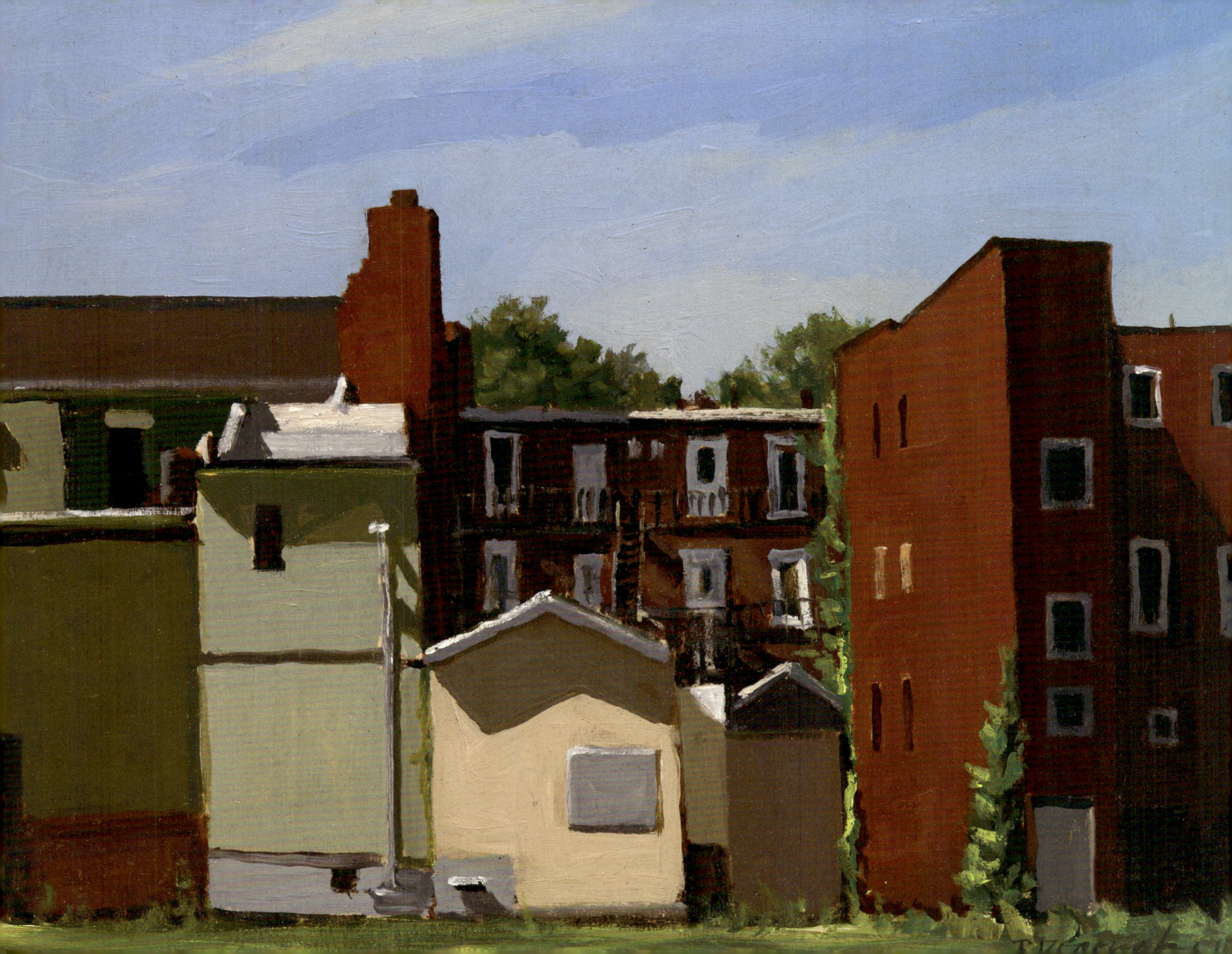

GUARDIAN

Union Township

An overgrown arborvitae tree seemed to guard this abandoned house. Weeds and vines also climb up the siding and onto the porch. In some odd way, there is a beauty to the slow decay of structures.

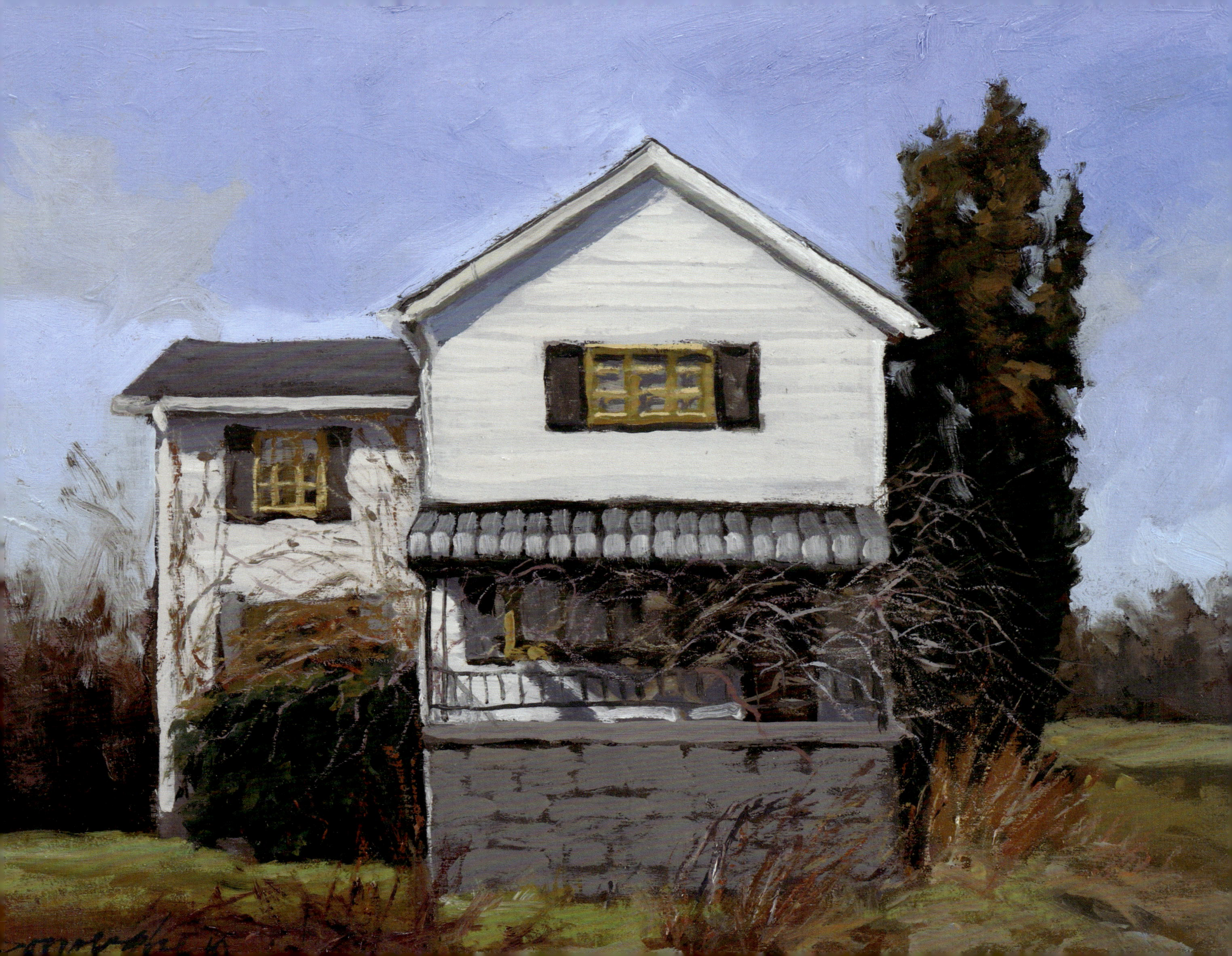

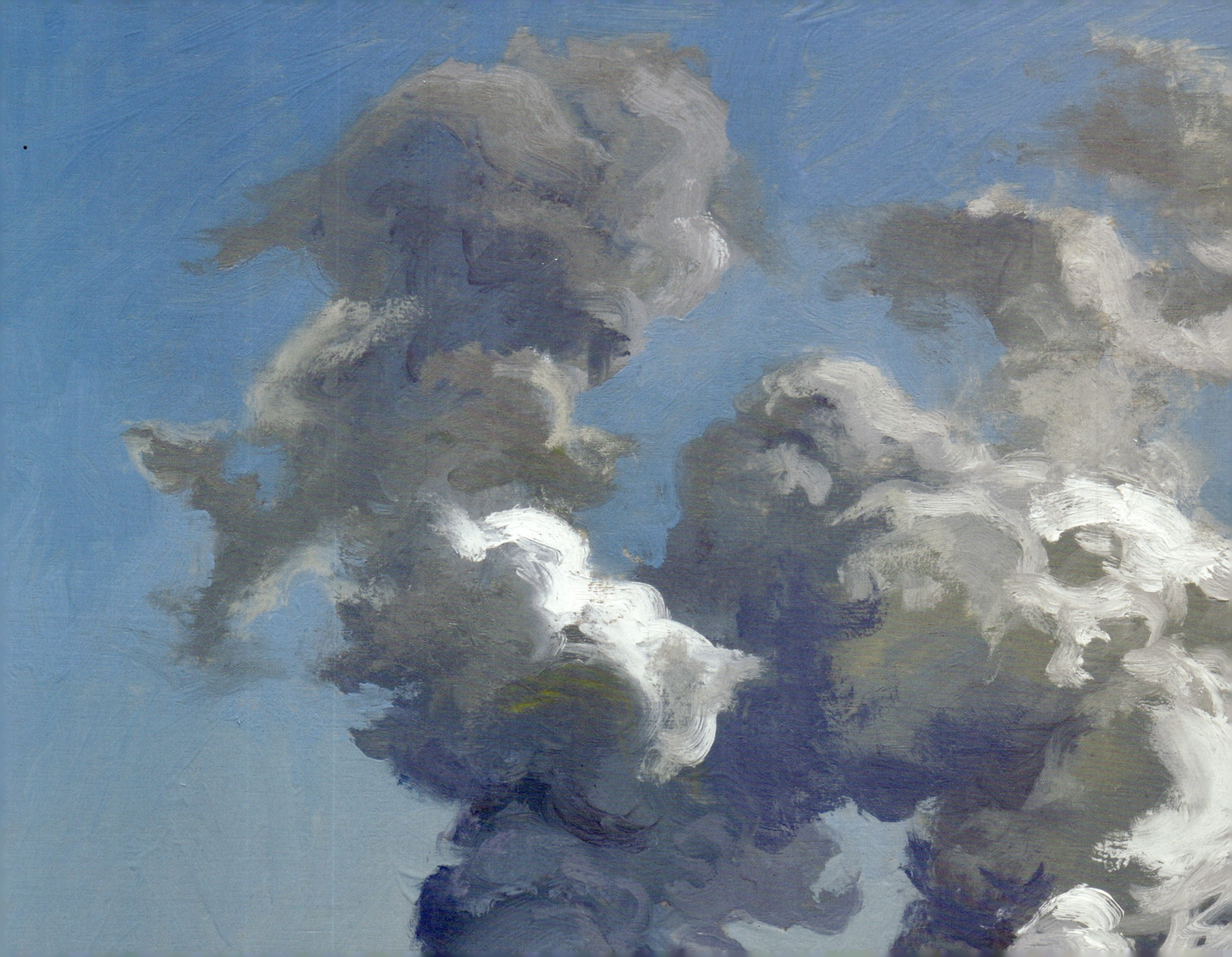

AISHA

Aisha has lived in Clairton all forty-six years of her life. She currently lives in a house that looks down on the mill where her cousin used to work. Until recently, she was a cheerleading coach at the high school. She says there's a lot of pride in Clairton. The town is very proud of the Bears football team. "I don't hate the mill. I don't hate it, but I don't love it. Our city was built from the steel mill from what I understand."

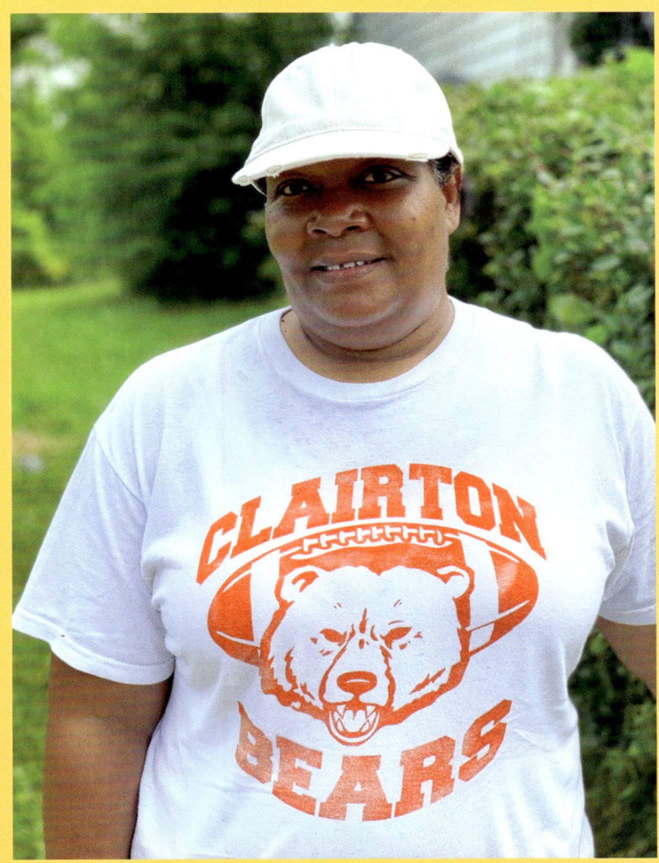

IMAGINARY PLUME

Courtney, view from New Eagle

The Mitchell Power Station ceased operation in 2013. I did this painting from the New Eagle Riverfront Park and added the plume later in my studio. It was easy to imagine the plume, but almost impossible to imagine meaningful development for a closed coal plant.

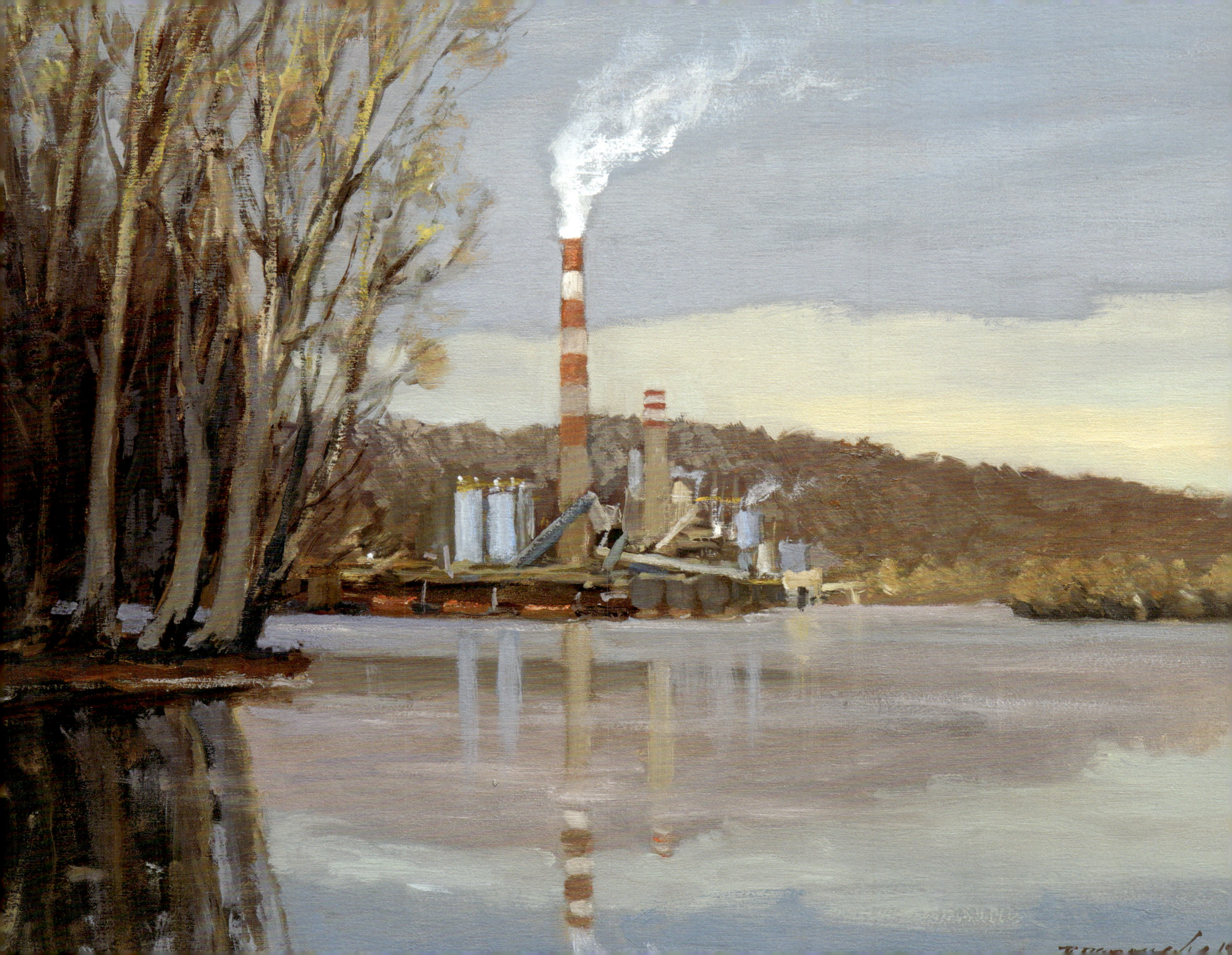

ELRAMA POWER PLANT

This hulking structure is one of two coal-fired plants that are closed along the Mon. Many factors contribute to the closing, including the large supply of natural gas, which is cleaner to burn. I was thinking about how that must have affected the local economy when a gentleman walked past. He started going on about the men he knew who had lost their jobs. Then he stopped, and without looking at me or the painting, stated with pride, "I know a lot of BS about this place."

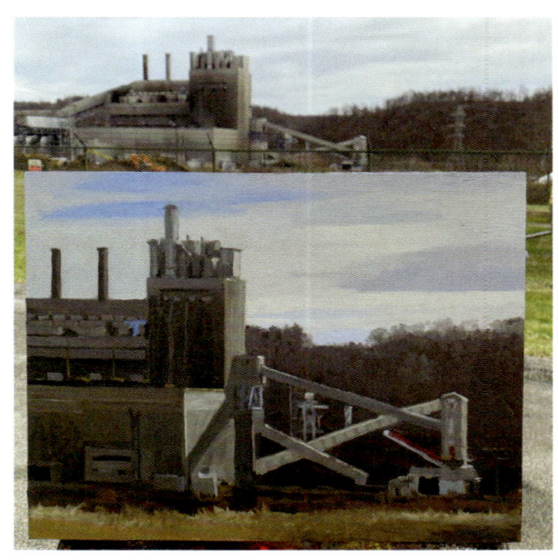

People aren't used to seeing an artist on their street, and many seemed curious or even suspicious. I feel like I'm an ambassador for the arts when on location and often chat with strangers to get a better understanding of a place and subject.

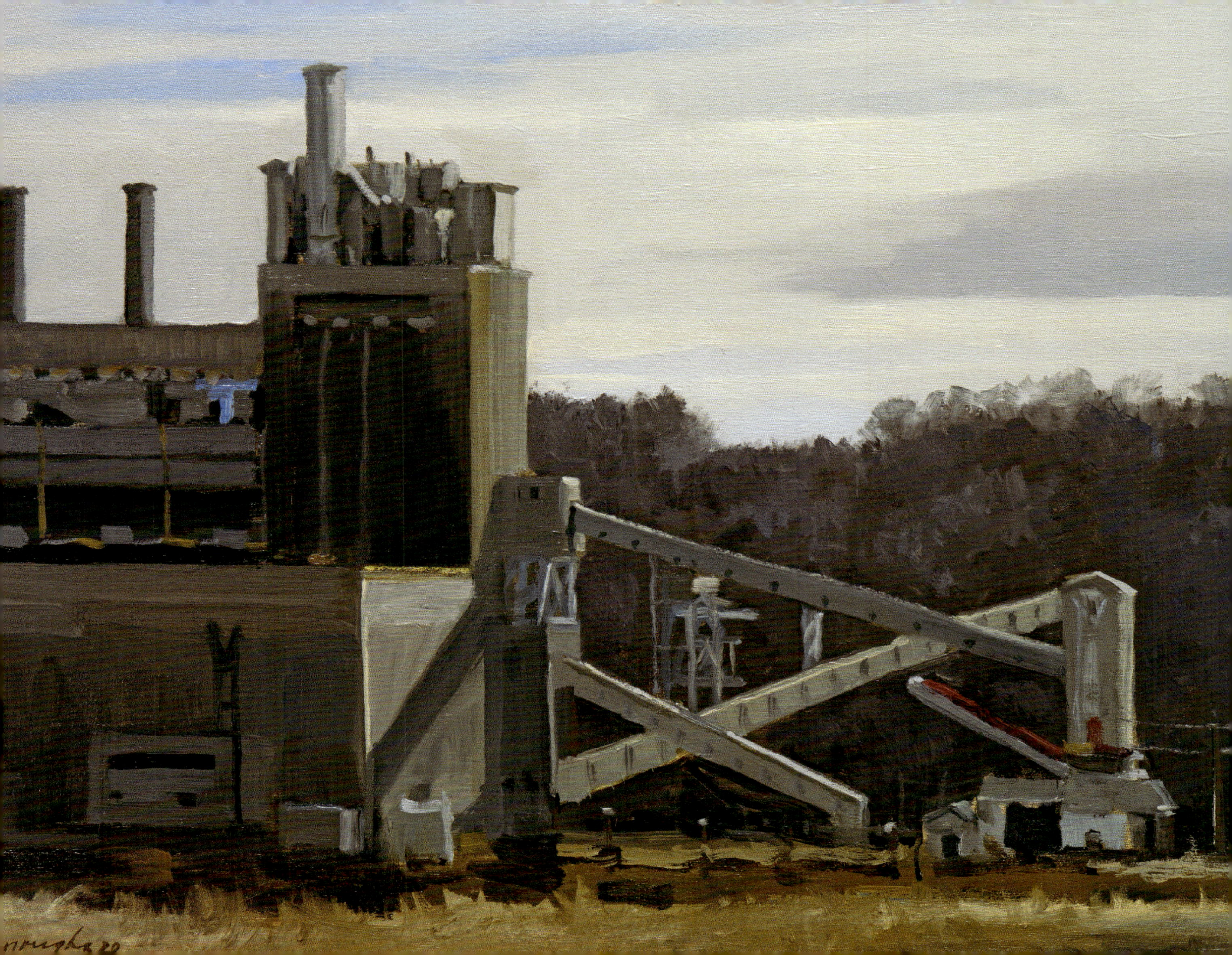

CHIMNEY POTS

Elizabeth

A window in the building directly behind me was open, but I didn't give it much thought because I was in a public parking lot. That is, until a woman stuck her head out only a few feet away to say she liked what I was doing.

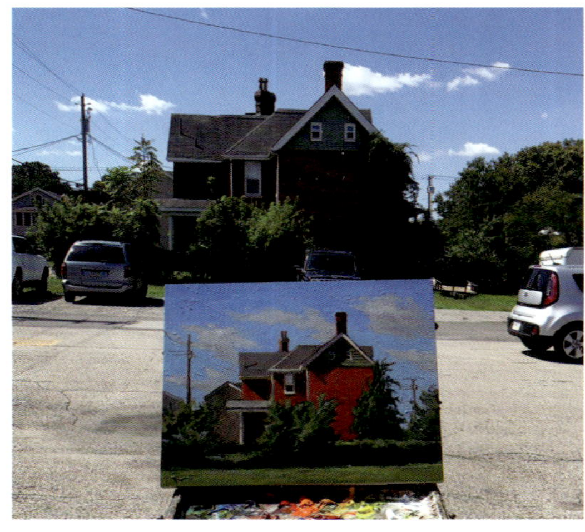

The town of Elizabeth has some wonderful old buildings. I'm especially drawn to brick houses that have such perfect proportions.

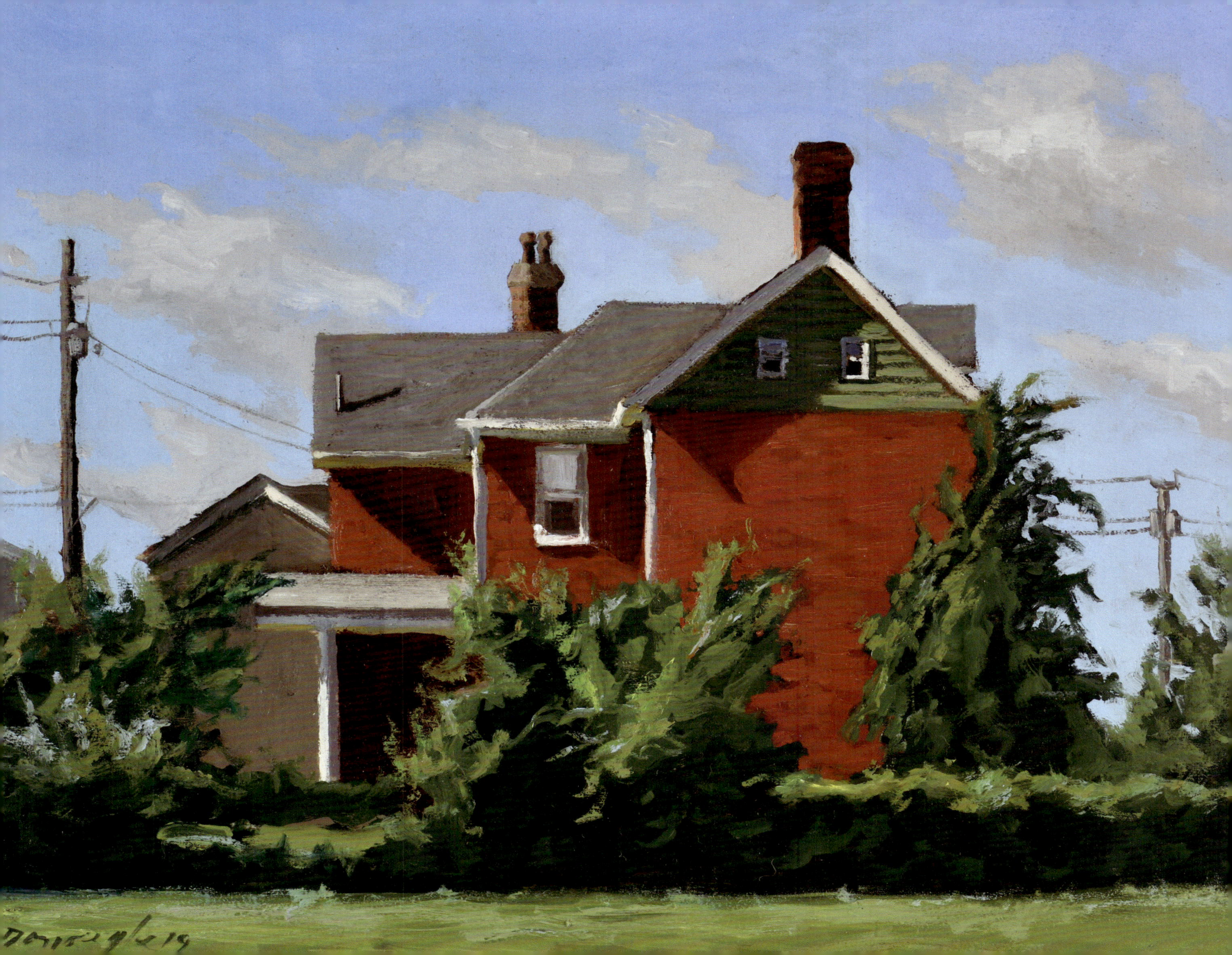

CLAIRTON PLUMES

Clairton

This was one of the first pieces completed in the series. There was a serious fire at this facility in early January of 2019, which caused air quality issues. I really noticed it as I mixed the many variations of gray for this painting.

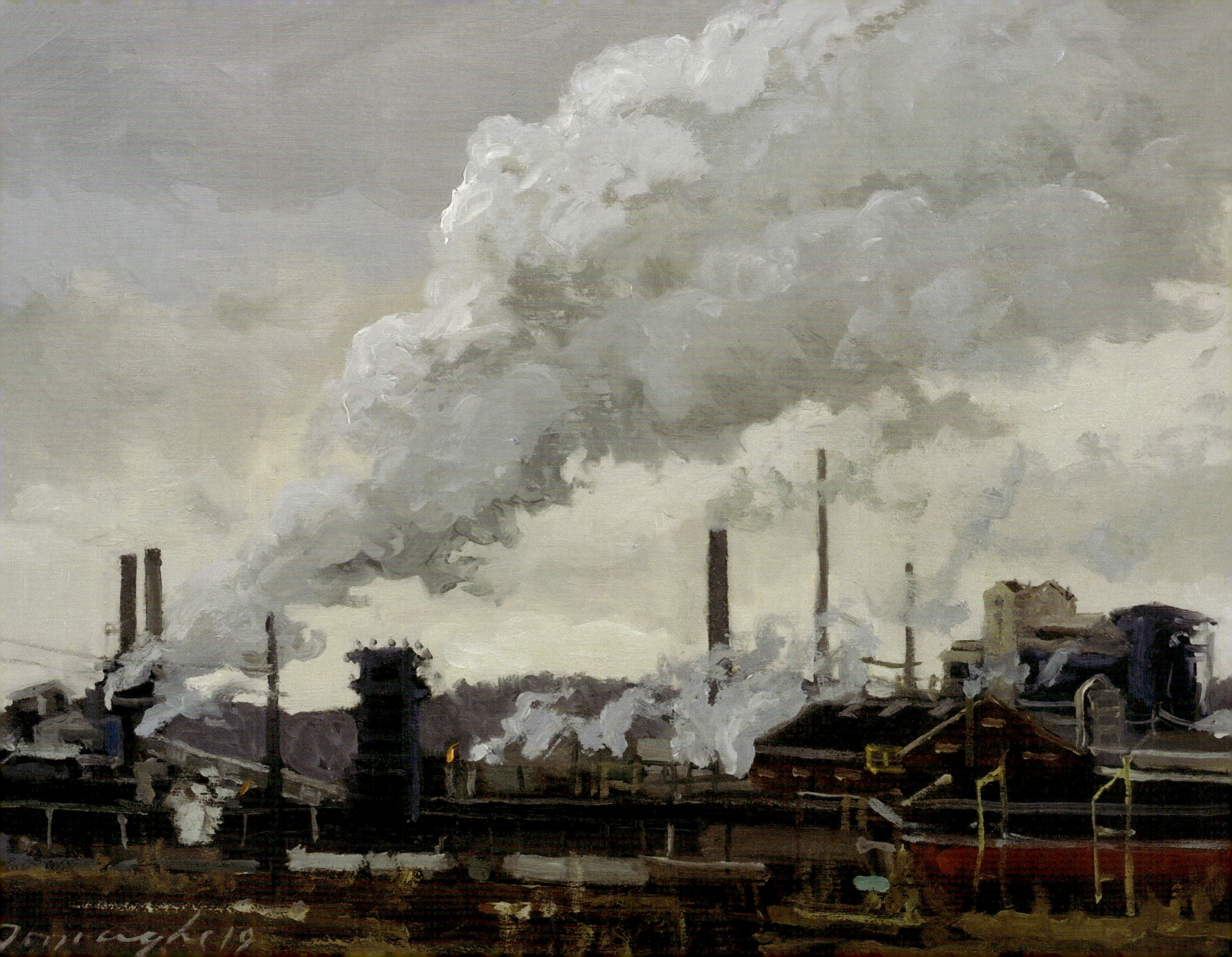

Donaghe 19

BARGES ON THE MON

Clairton, view from West Mifflin

It's possible I was trespassing when I painted this classic scene. It's important to be on location to get the spirit of a place. The barges on the Mon are quite poetic as they quietly move materials through the water.

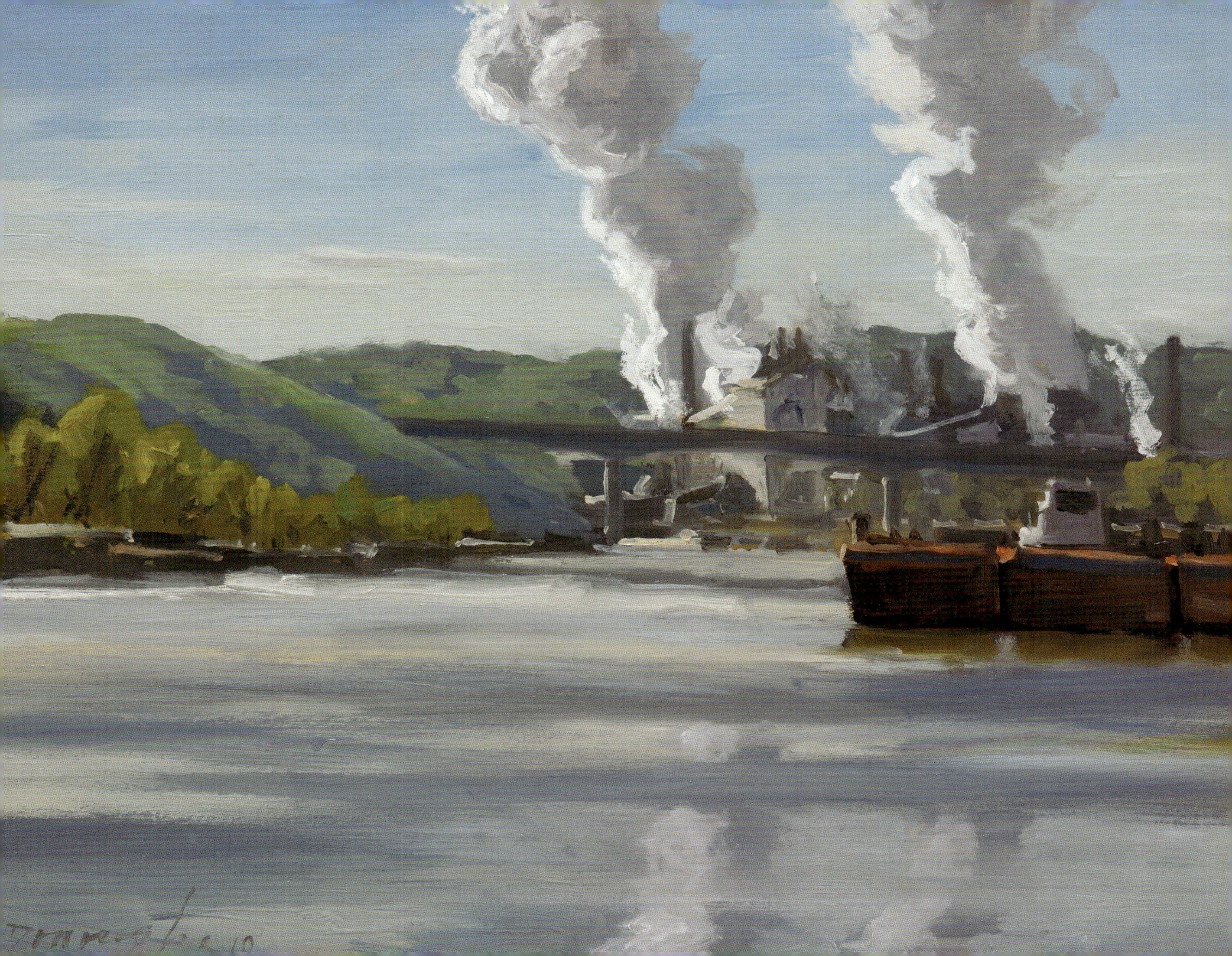

COAL FOR COKE

Clairton

One of my early memories is of accompanying my father to the nearby rail yards. He worked for the railroad for over forty years. Seeing these cars loaded with bituminous coal recalls a way of life I experienced in Cambria County, Pennsylvania.

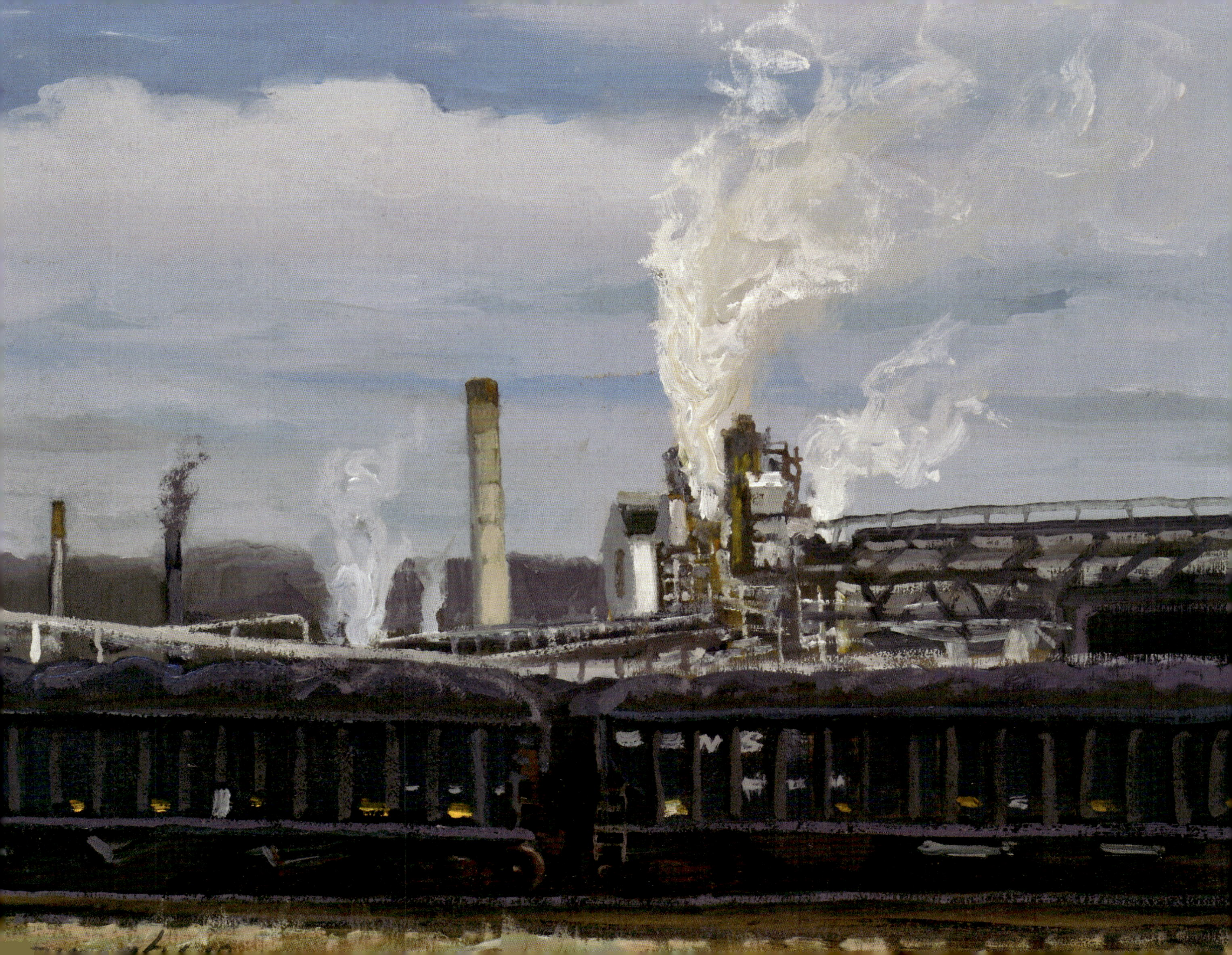

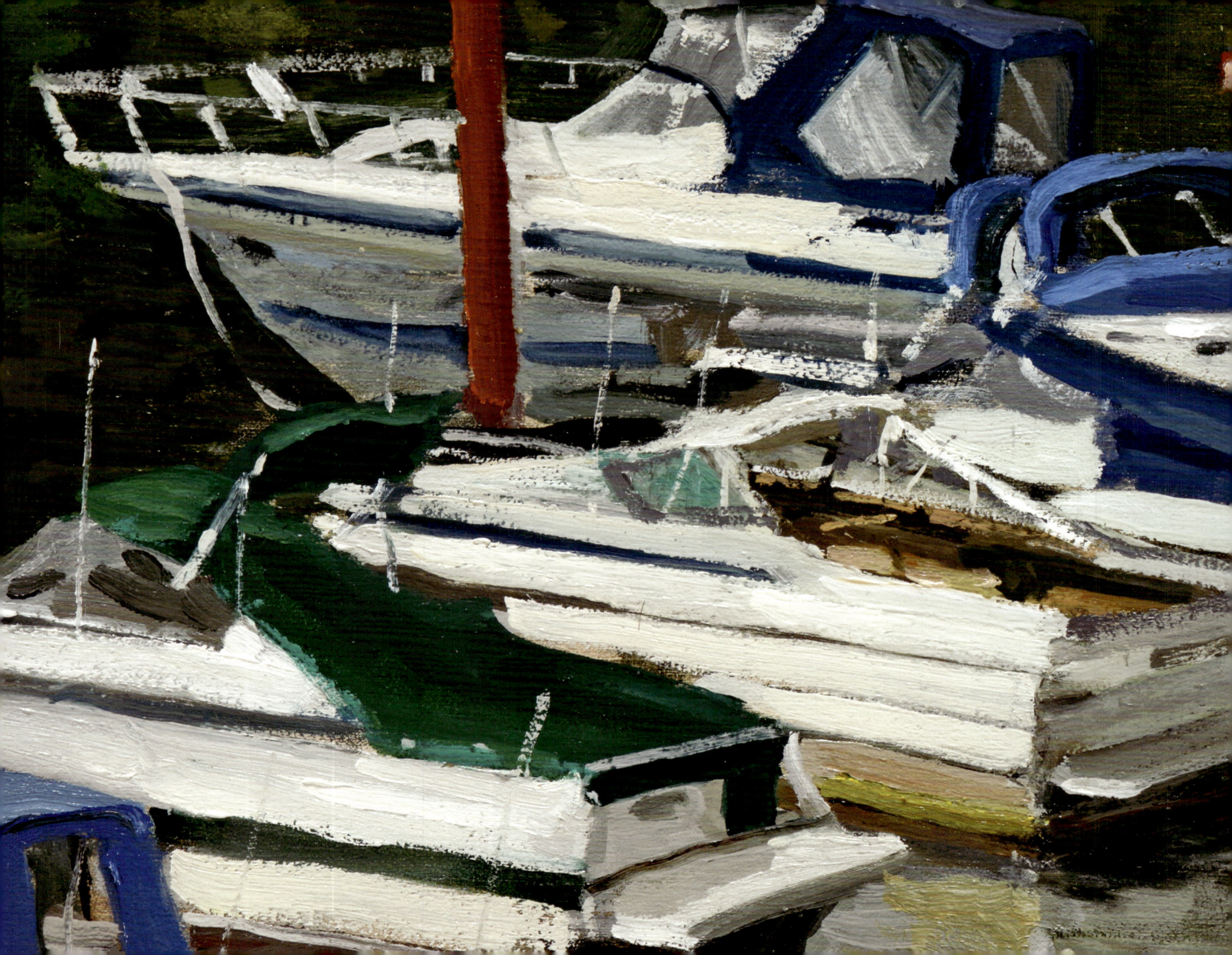

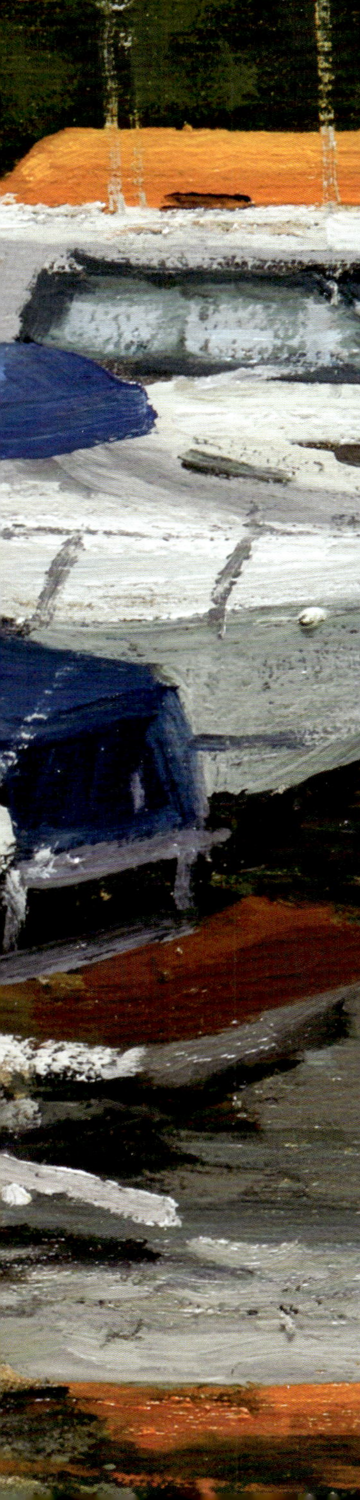

HAROLD

Harold is twenty-six years old and lives in Jefferson Hills Borough and works as a home healthcare aid. He recently became engaged and plans to marry in the fall of 2021. He says there are good signs about what's happening in the area, but says people here are struggling and dealing with poverty. He graduated from Clairton High School, where he met his fiancée. Harold says new homes in that area are bringing beauty back to the neighborhood. He likes to go fishing in Elizabeth Borough and caught a sheepshead on the day this photo was taken. "I think as far as poverty and employment, it has been an issue and will continue to be an issue."

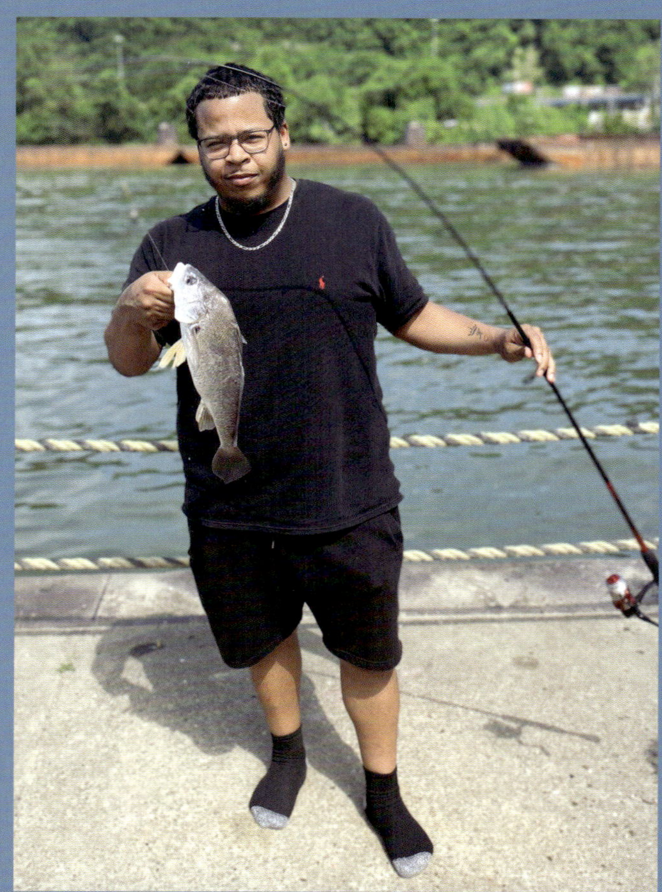

COKE PRODUCTION

Clairton

The production of steel relies on high-quality coke and the Clairton plant is one of the largest producers of coke in the United States. It's also a throwback to the industrial age of the Pittsburgh region when coal was also used for heating. Old-timers talk about changing their white shirts twice a day because of the particulates.

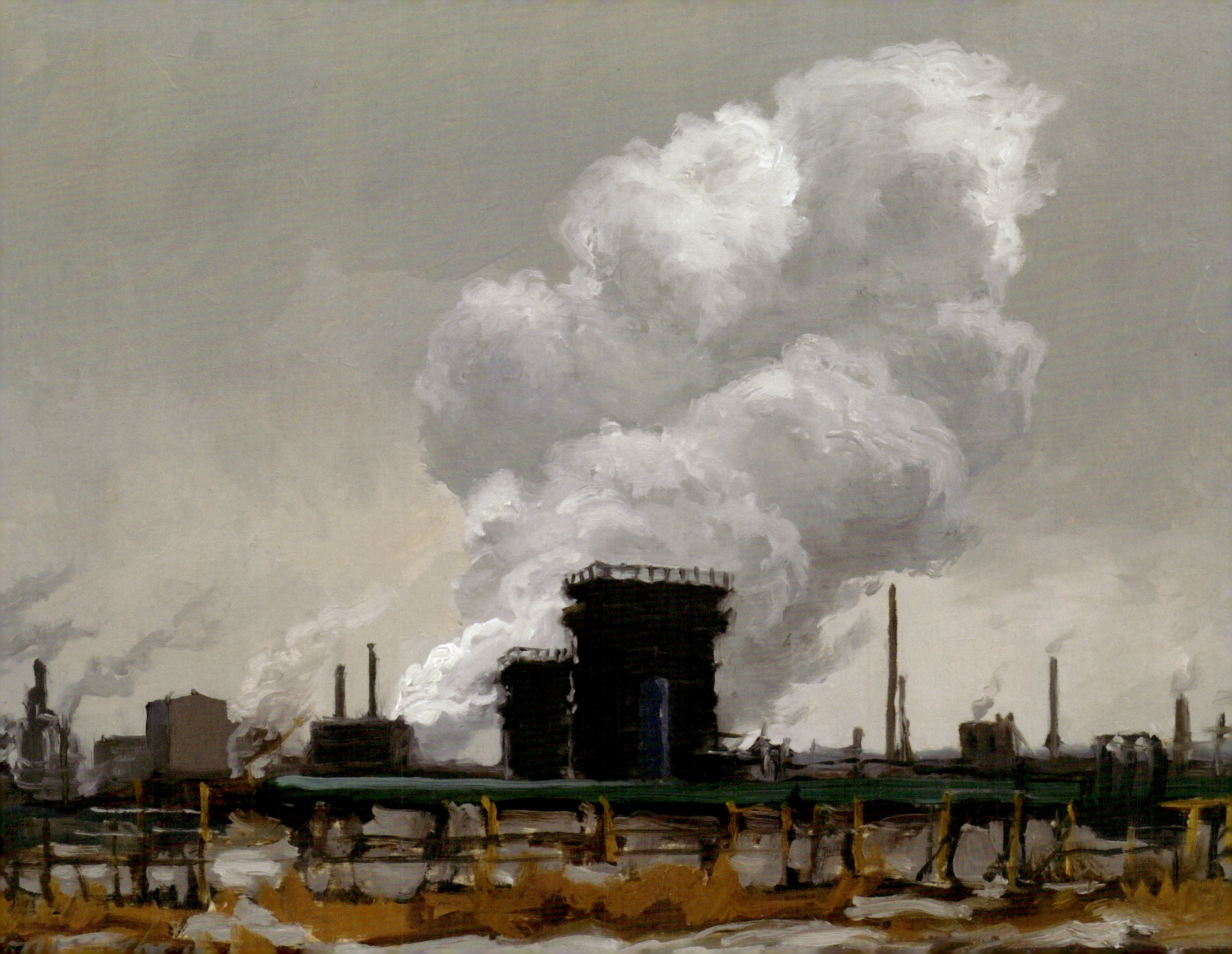

SHADOW OF A MILL

Clairton

Morning light on these American foursquare houses and the plumes behind them inspired this painting. Common scenes such as this defined much of the Mon Valley for decades. It reminded me how industry and those who toiled were closely aligned.

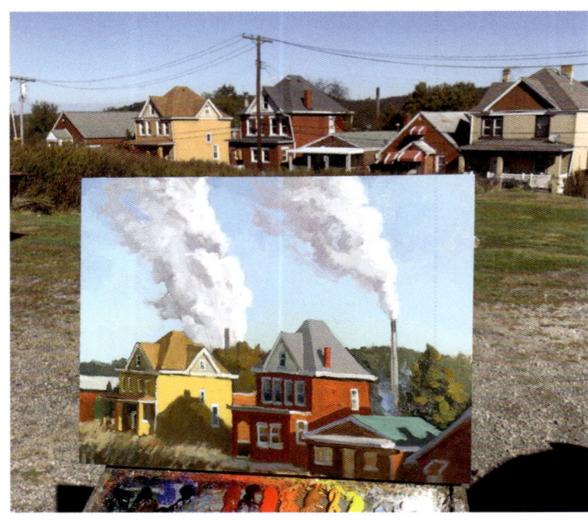

I imagine this as a classic Mon Valley scene, and it's exactly what I was searching for as I traveled the valley.

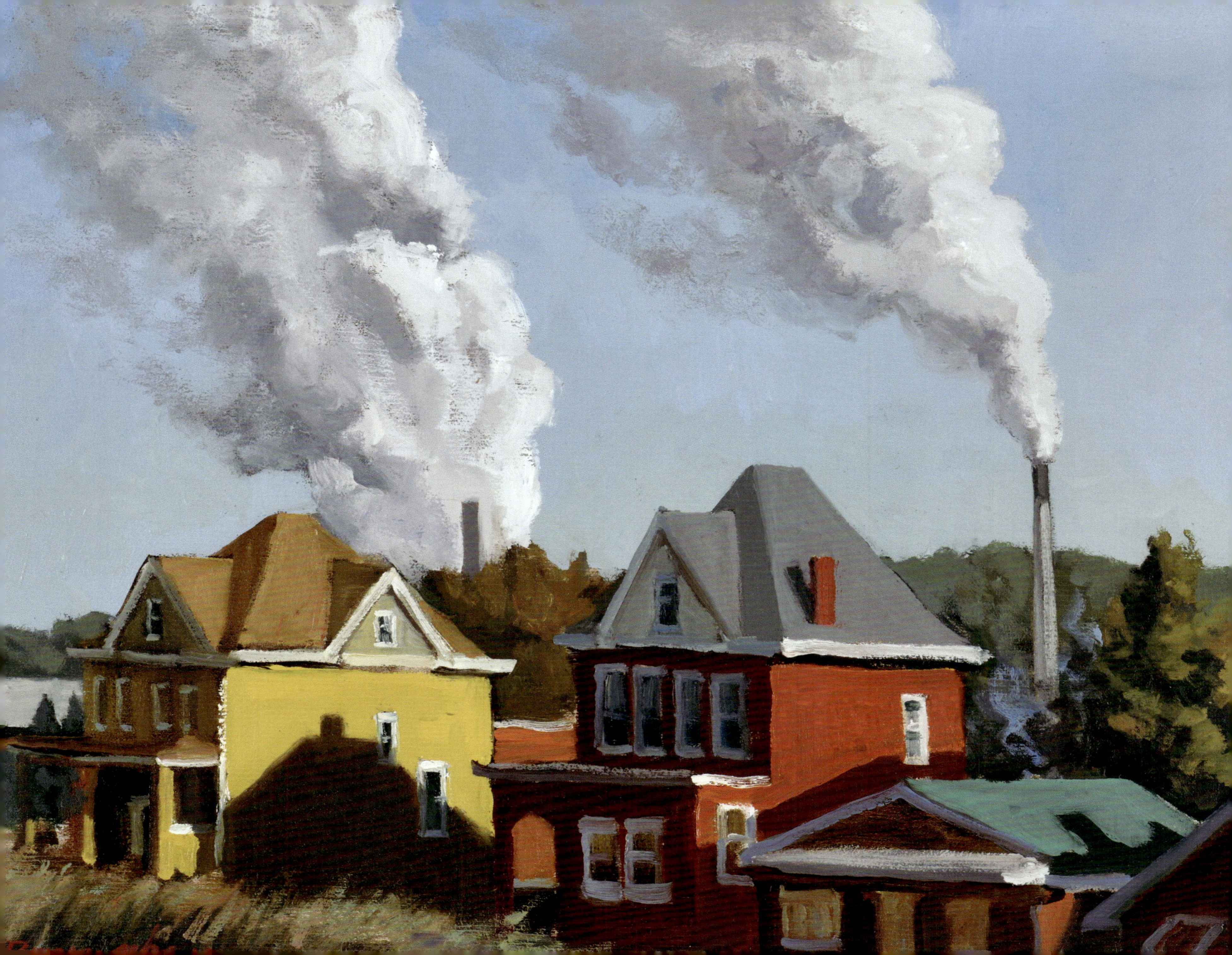

TWIN RELEASE

Clairton

The United States Steel Corporation Clairton Plant offers a spectacular visual display. The "quenching process" creates gigantic vapor plumes that fill the sky with twisting, cloudlike formations. This plant sits on the west bank of the Monongahela River just twenty miles south of Pittsburgh.

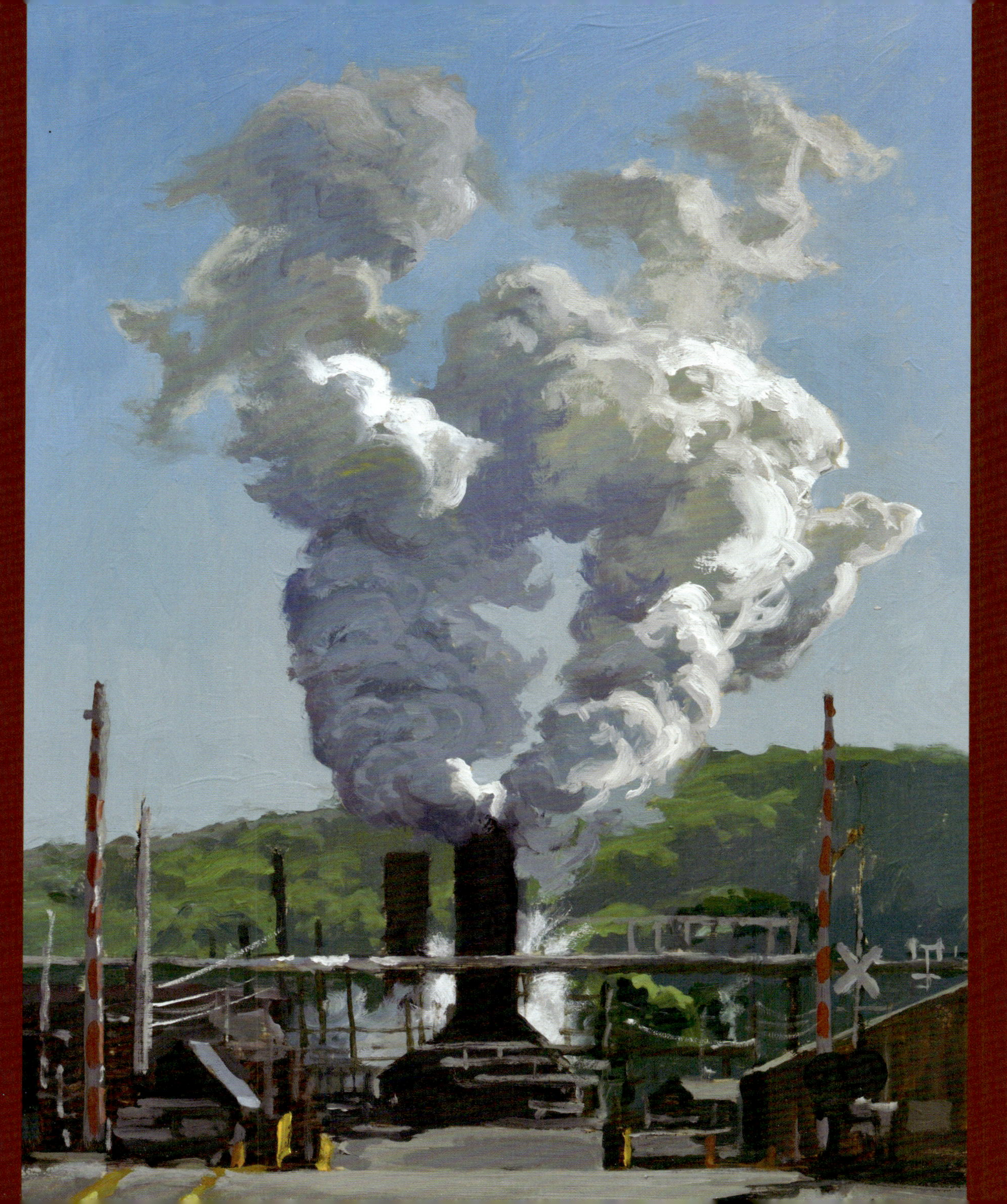

MON WINTER

Glassport, view from Clairton

These structures caught my eye every time I drove along the river. They were obviously built to accommodate the Monongahela River commerce. The river was once a superhighway—when not frozen over. The pioneers used this route when they came from New England to settle the west. Pittsburgh was a destination for travelers venturing west on the Ohio River.

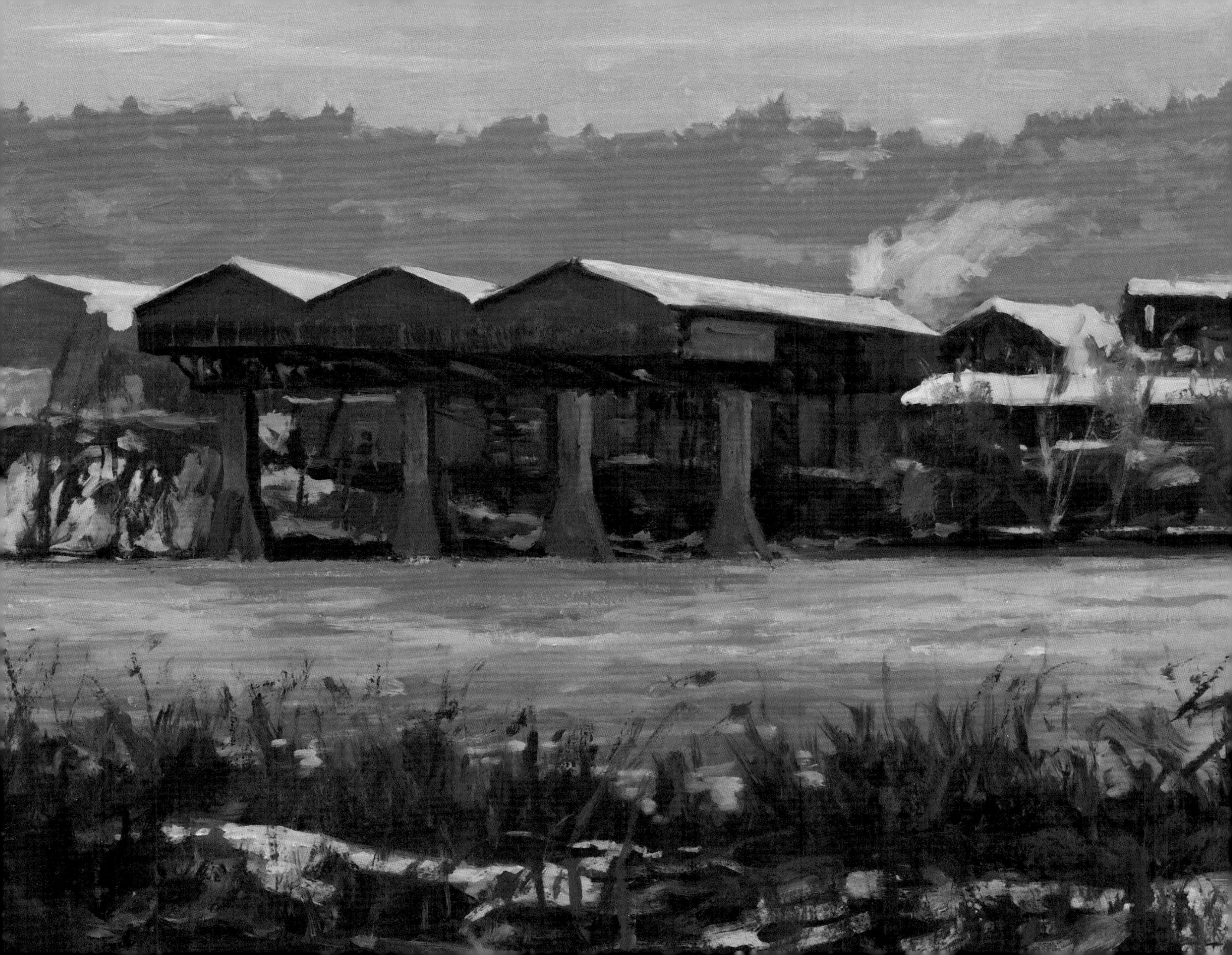

WAREHOUSES

Glassport

The Mon Valley has many warehouses; some look like they could be from another era. Nature and the passage of time creeps back to take what it wants. The tree that made it way through these buildings reminded me of this fact.

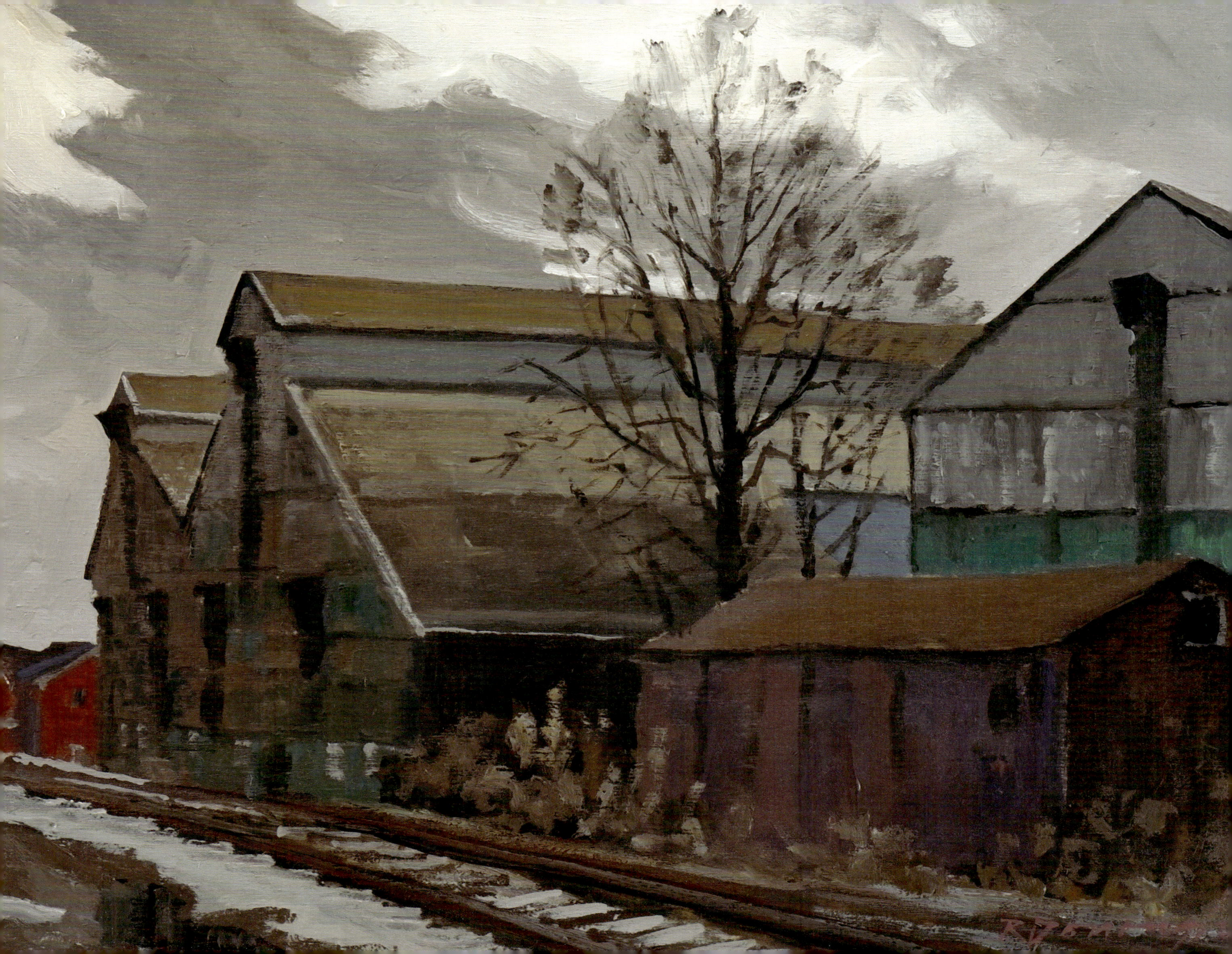

6TH STREET VISTA

McKeesport

Many homes stand alone because others have been razed. It gives a rather isolated feeling because we're used to seeing homes beside each other, especially in town. On this wet day, though, it was easy to see the distant hillside homes that flanked this handsome house.

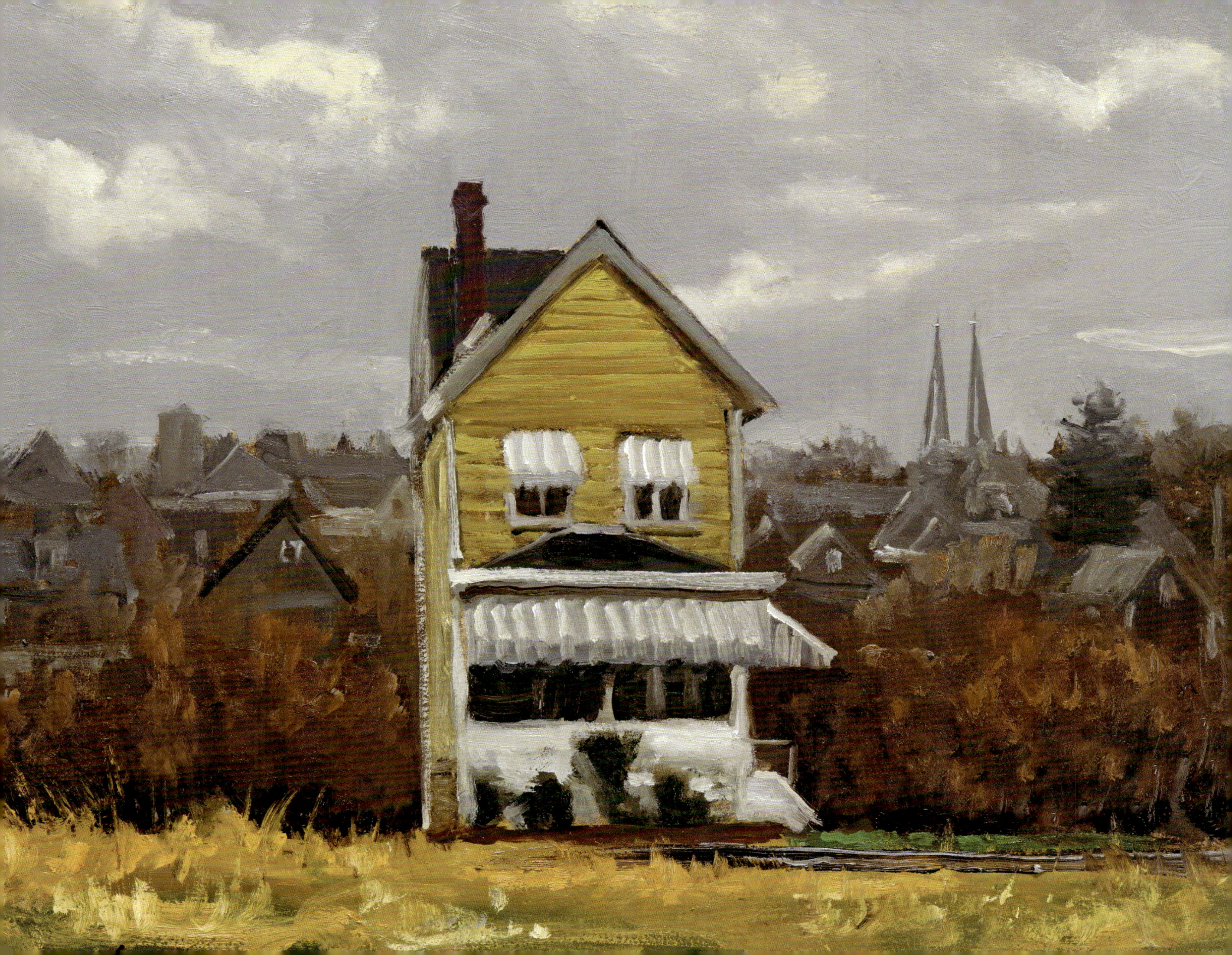

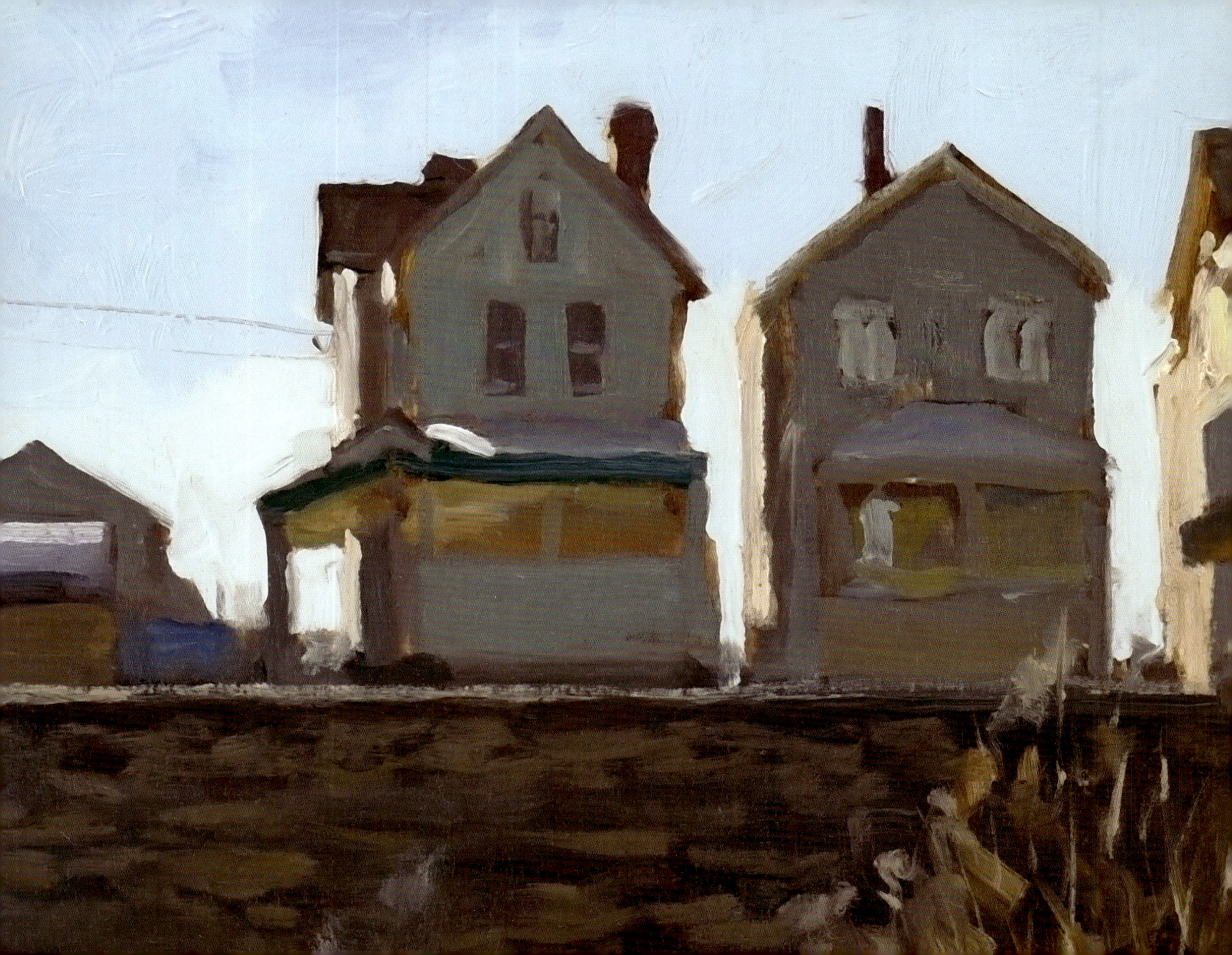

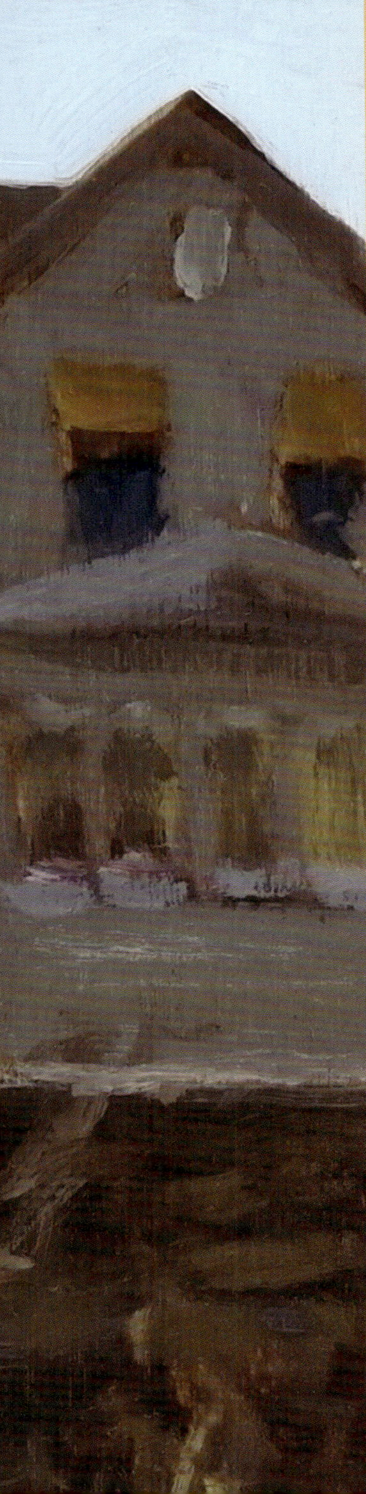

MELISSA AND SAM

Melissa grew up in the Little Boston section of McKeesport and now lives in the Mount Vernon part of town. She thinks downtown McKeesport can make a change and get better, but she's not optimistic about other parts of town. She works as a dental assistant at the Pittsburgh Veterans Affairs Medical Center in Oakland. She lives with her partner, Sam, and they enjoy riding his motorcycle together. He grew up in Greenfield and moved to McKeesport about twenty-five years ago after buying a home in the town. "Maybe there will be a turnaround up here. Friendly people around. That's why I stay."

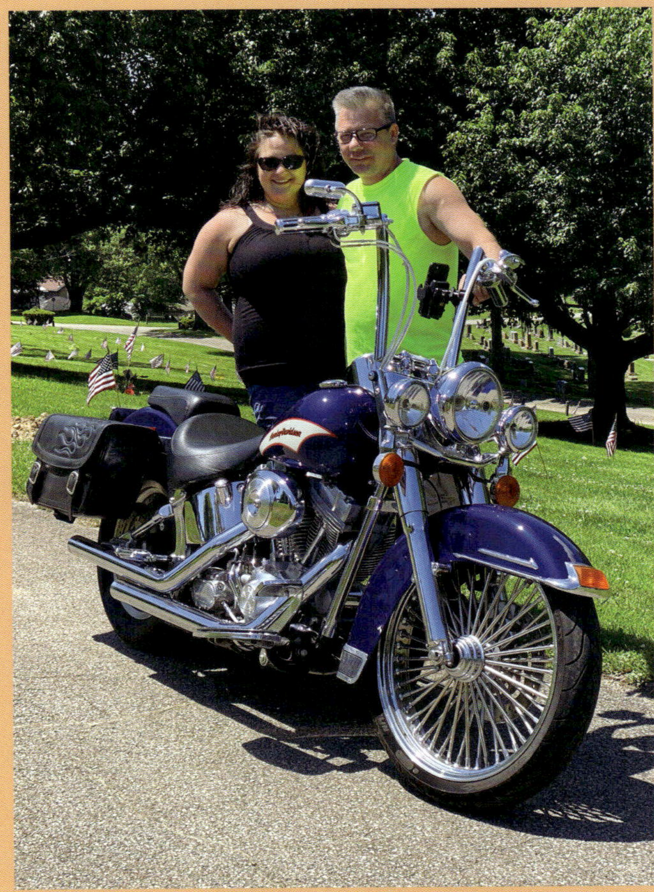

AUTUMN CEMETERY

McKeesport

Founded in 1856, The McKeesport and Versailles Cemetery offers some very interesting and historic monuments. Sadly, many are damaged. It is still worth a visit to explore an area where it is said that American Indian chiefs were laid to rest.

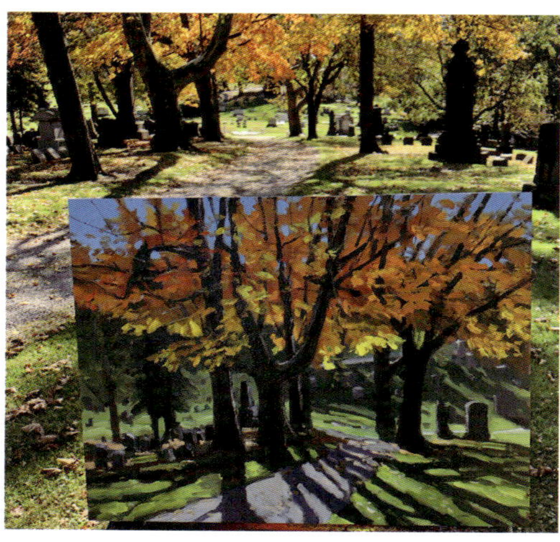

The autumn is a glorious time to be outdoors. I noticed quite a few folks walking the cemetery to enjoy its quiet beauty.

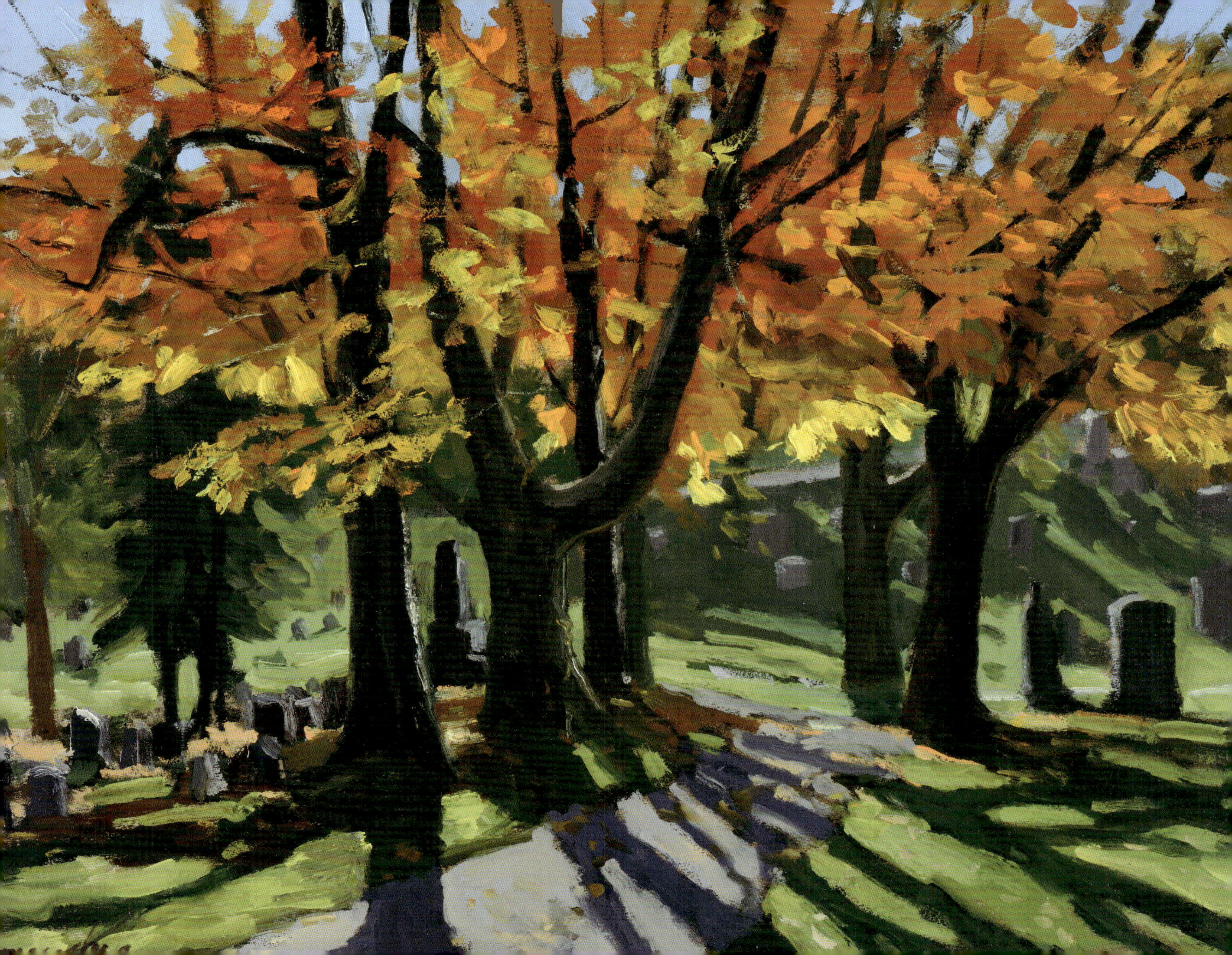

GERGELY RIVERFRONT PARK

Public parks give so much joy. I've enjoyed painting in parks because they are a window to the soul. The day I did this I watched disabled folks sit quietly in the sun and talk. It was so peaceful.

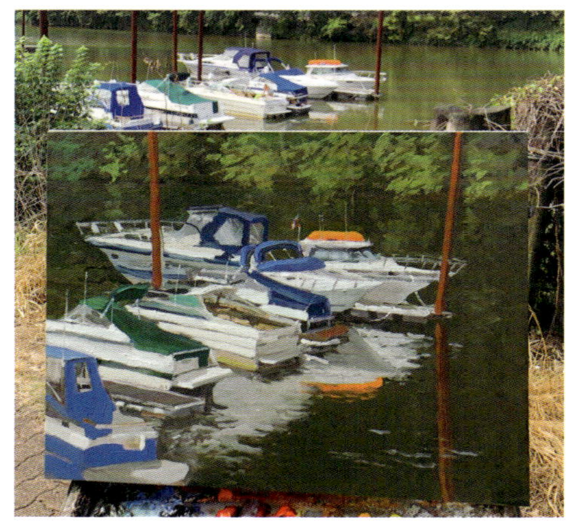

Water recreation is a big part of the Mon Valley. It is obvious that many people enjoy the river. About halfway through this painting, I noticed a couple boarding their boat. Sadly for them, the motor wouldn't turn over, which allowed me to complete the piece.

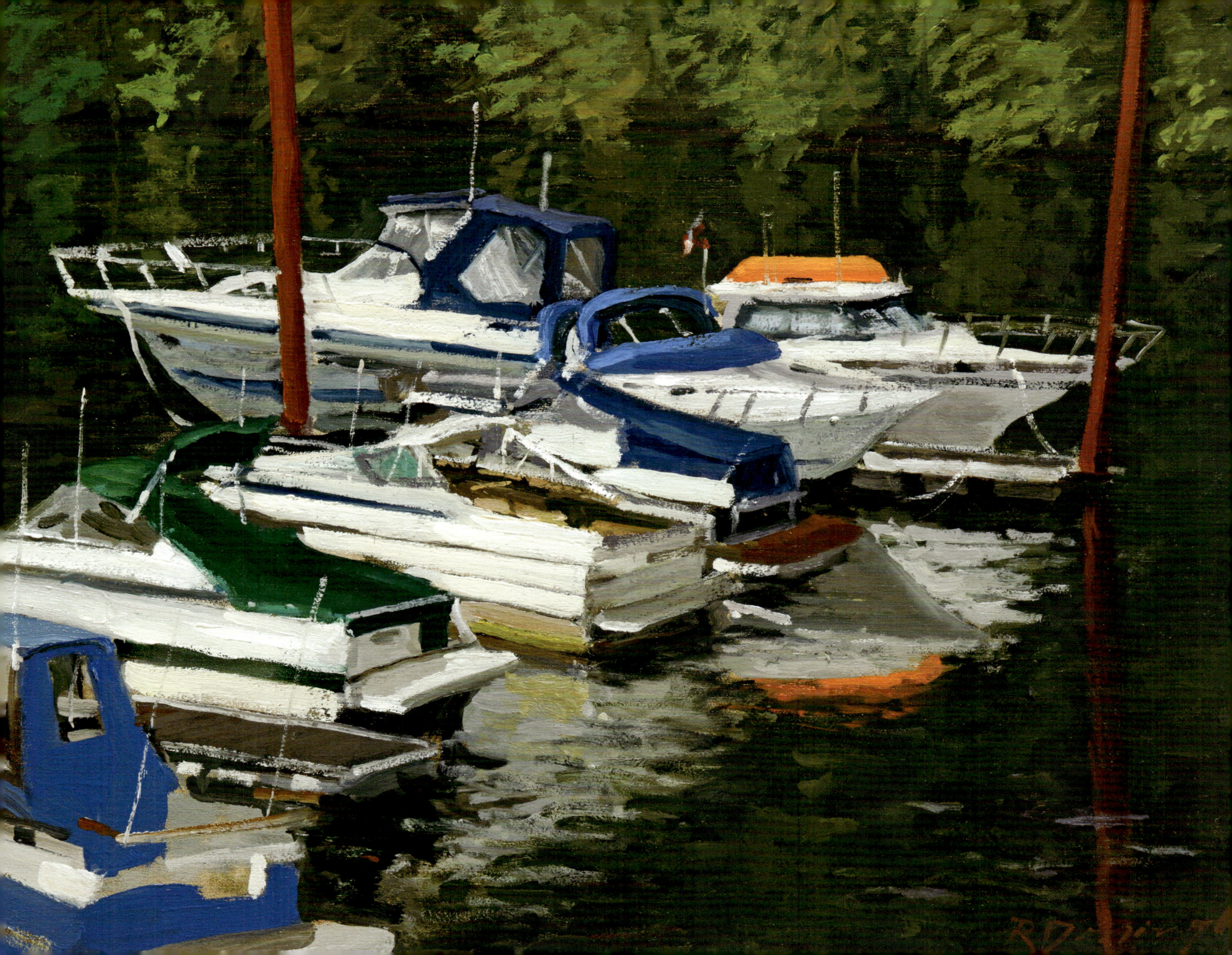

MCKEESPORT CONNECTING ROUNDHOUSE

This historic structure was once used as a machine shop for repairing locomotives. It sits in stark contrast to the nearby shiny new buildings. It dates to the early 1900s and still has a lot of charm even though it is currently abandoned.

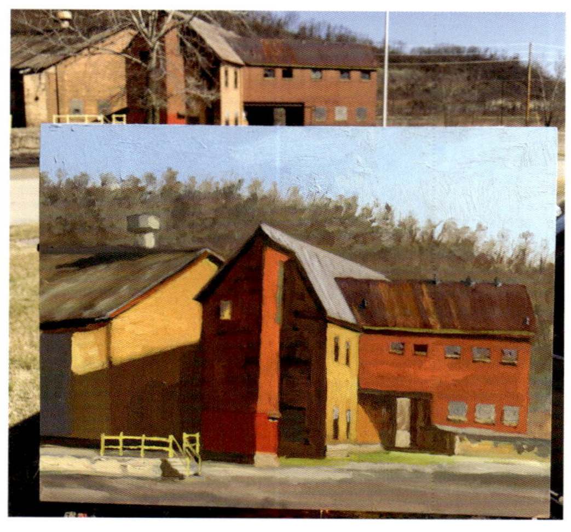

Often, I'm influenced by the light and shadow, and the play of warm against cool colors. This particular building had all of that, plus a unique geometry.

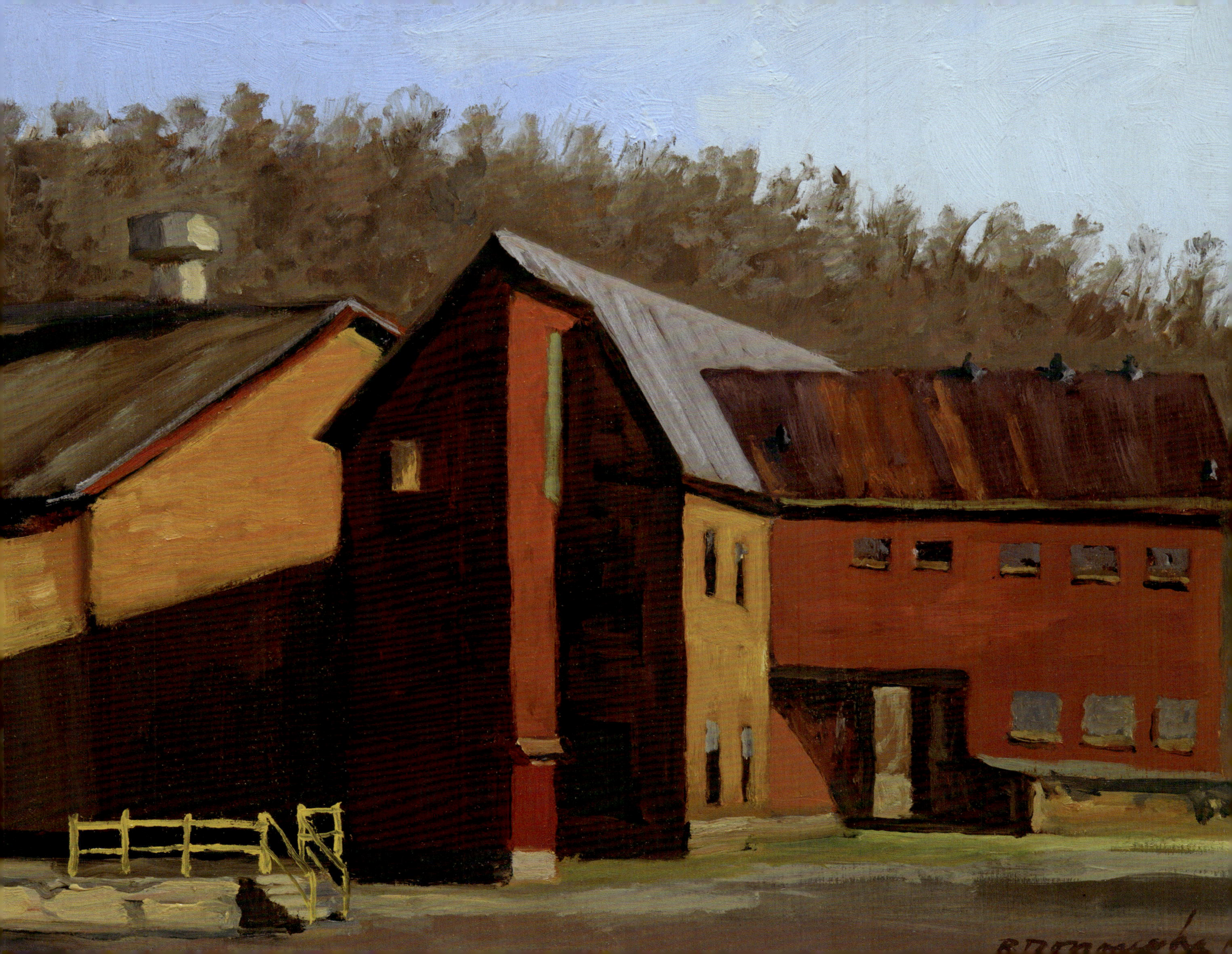

MCKEESPORT NEIGHBORS

McKeesport

This steep hillside was mostly in shadow on this winter morning. There is a lot of unexpected beauty that can be found in shadow areas. The silhouettes of the houses made for an interesting contrast to the bleak hillside below.

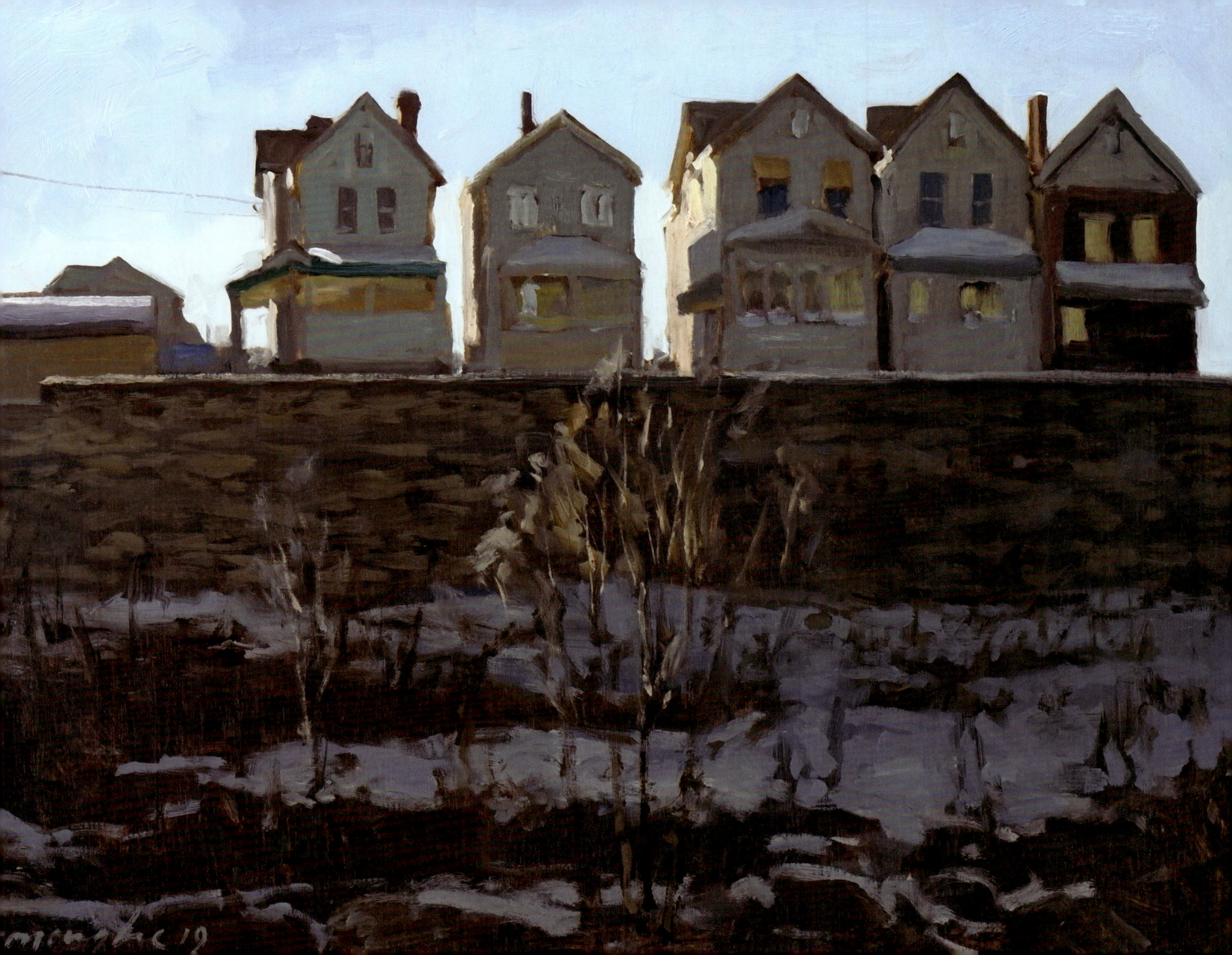

PIPE MANUFACTURING

McKeesport became known as "Tube City" after United States Steel acquired National Tube in 1901. The repetitive geometry of the pipes seemed to echo the long horizontal shape of the warehouses, while the vertical lights added a perpendicular contrast.

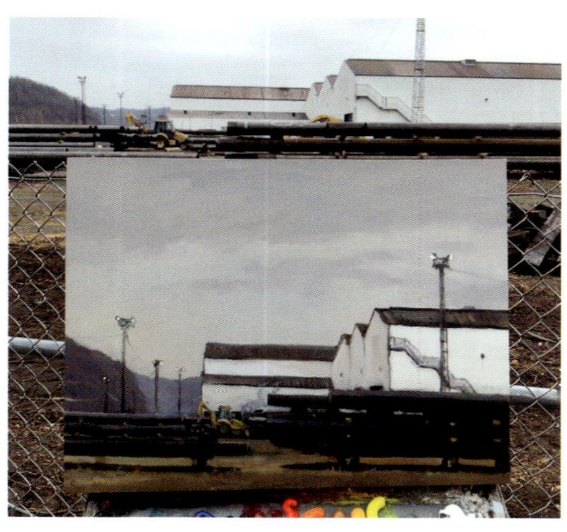

The walking trail along the river provided a nice view of this plant. Pipes were being moved and welded as I worked.

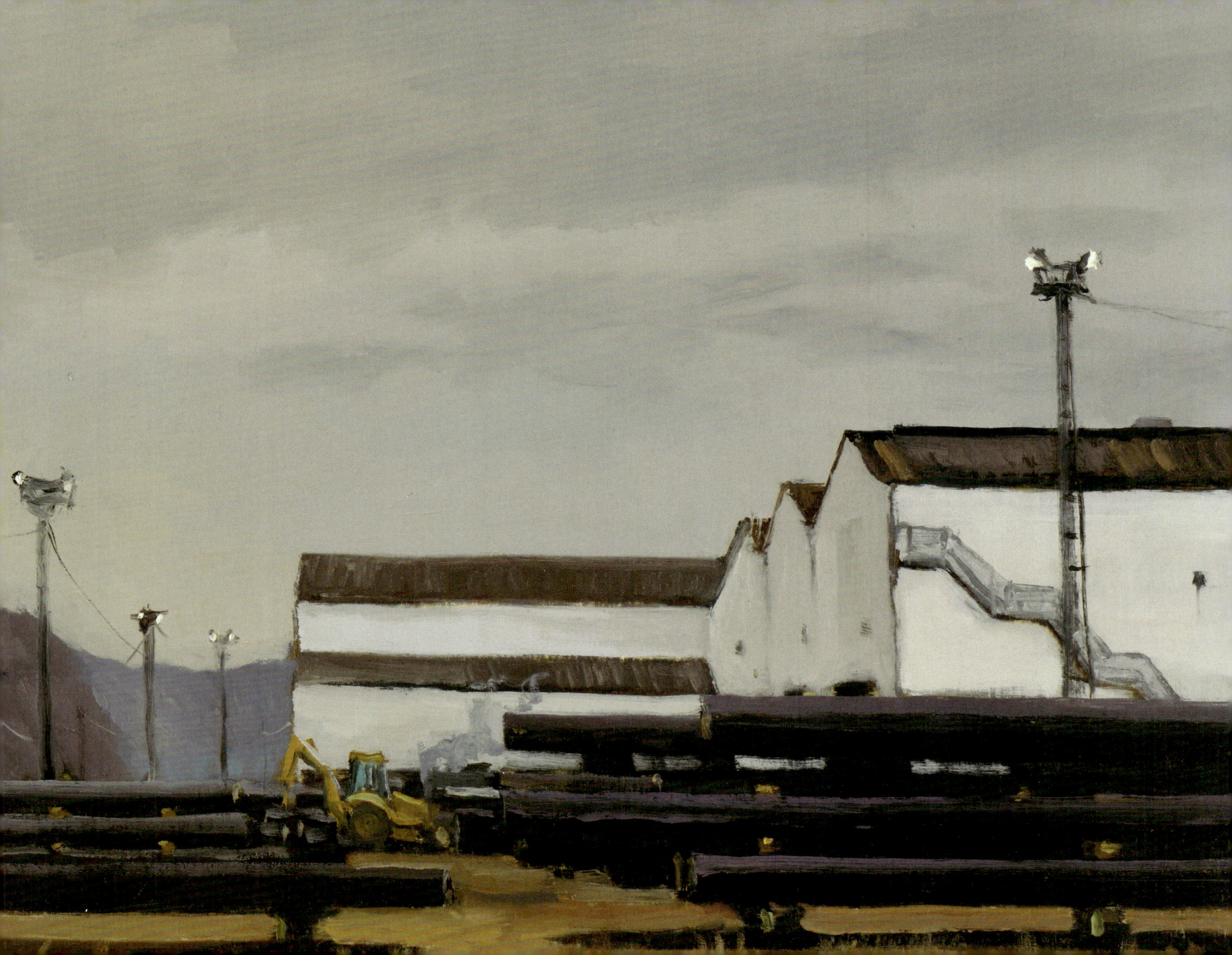

ABANDONED

Duquesne

There are many abandoned structures in need of repair. As nature reclaims what man once built, there is a sad beauty. Here the nearby wires were also being invaded by vines and weeds

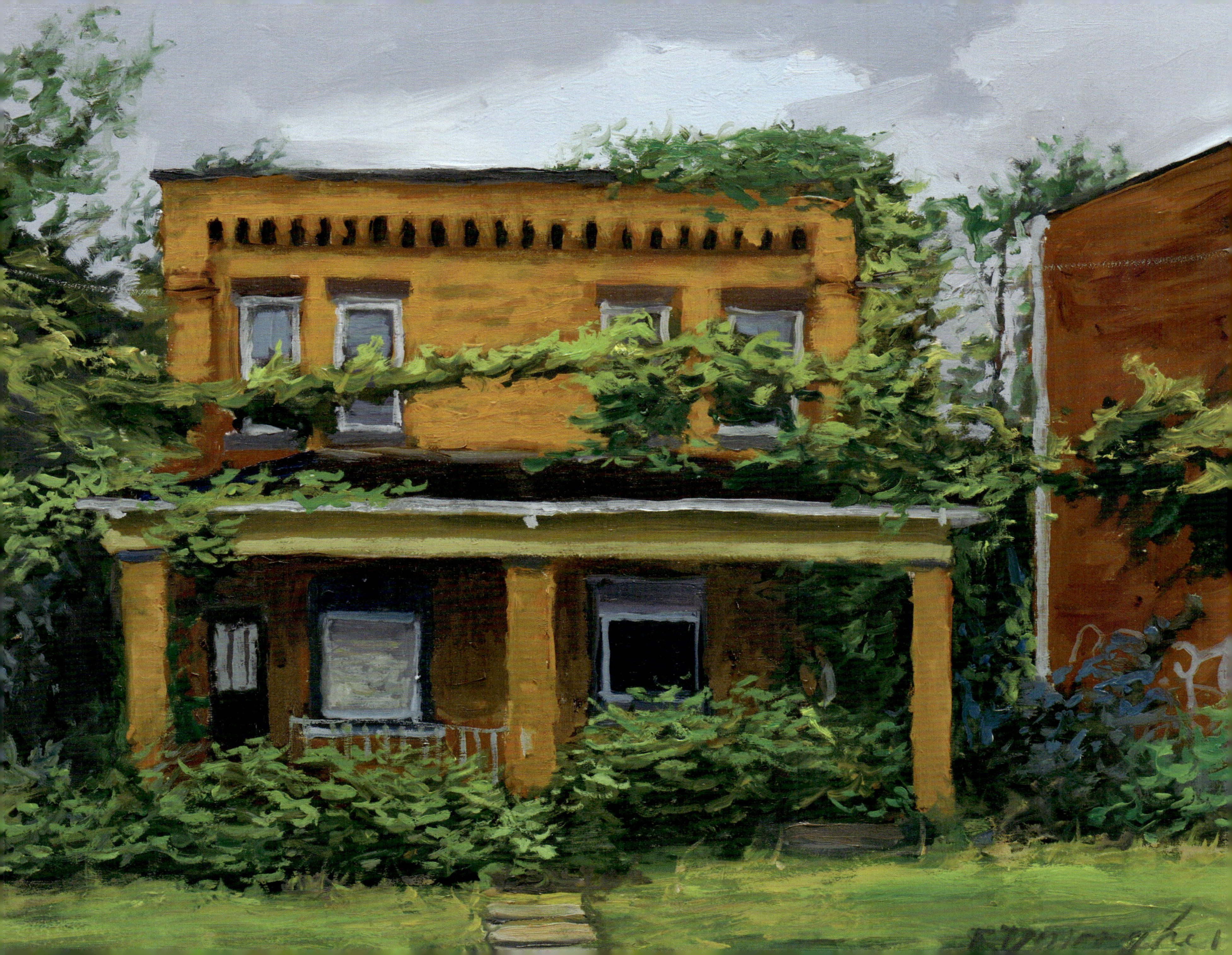

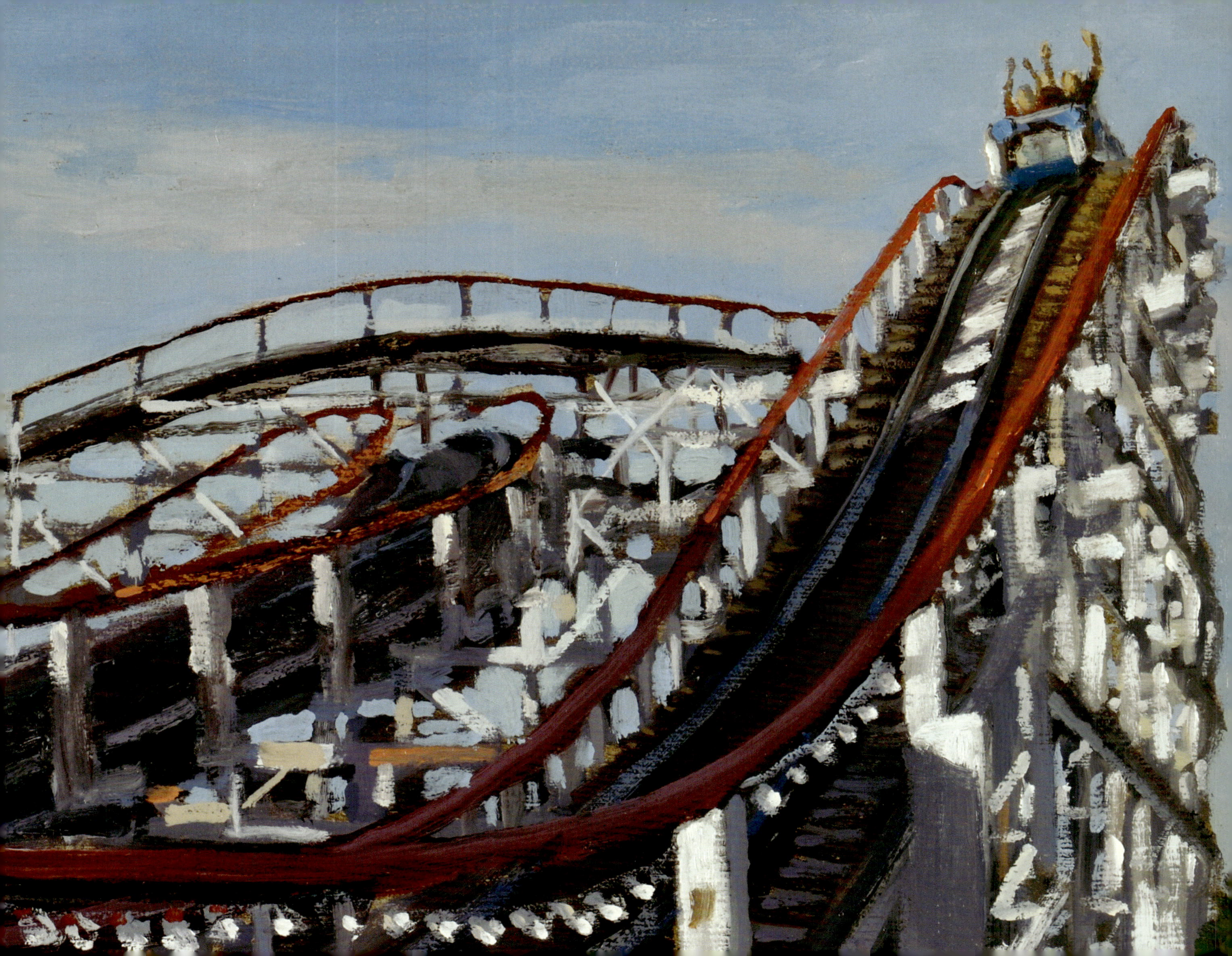

AMIRAH

Amirah is thirteen years old and excited to be going into eighth grade in fall 2020 in the West Mifflin Area School District. She lives with her mother in Duquesne and enjoys hanging out with her friends. She says she hopes being featured in this project makes her famous. Her mother moved to the neighborhood about ten years ago, but Amirah spent the last few years going to school in the Kiski Area School District because she was living in that area with her father. "There are things to do here and fun space to walk around. There's interesting people here. Like, really interesting. It's okay. I want to go to Florida for the beaches and the weather. I've been down there on vacation."

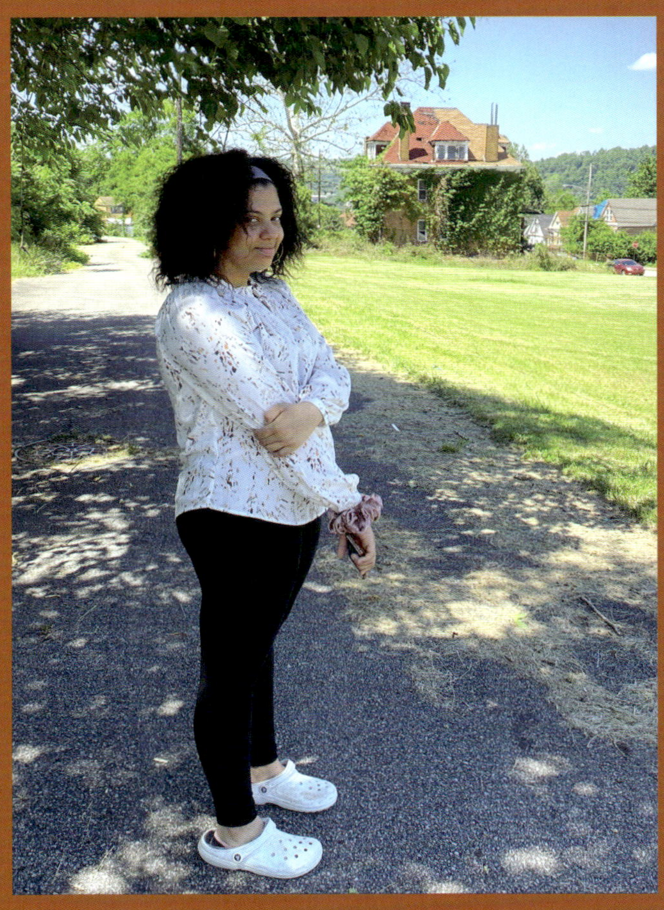

SOUTH SECOND STREET DUQUESNE

Duquesne

There are times when I have absolutely no idea what I'll paint. Then all of a sudden, a subject calls out to be painted. This yellow brick house in Duquesne had a rather quiet dignity that felt strong against the gray-violet sky.

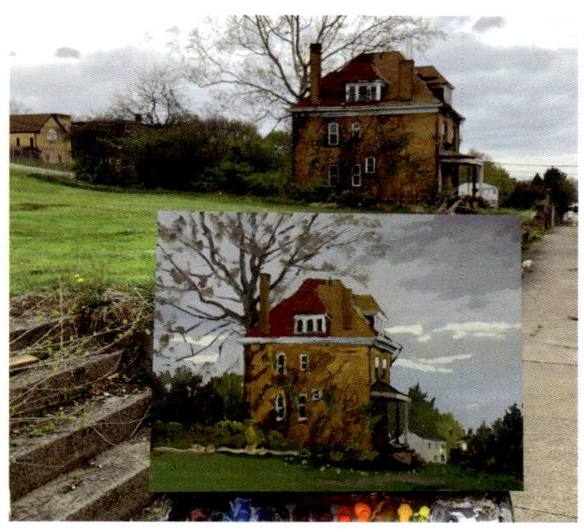

Neighbors watched this painting take shape from the privacy of their house across the street.

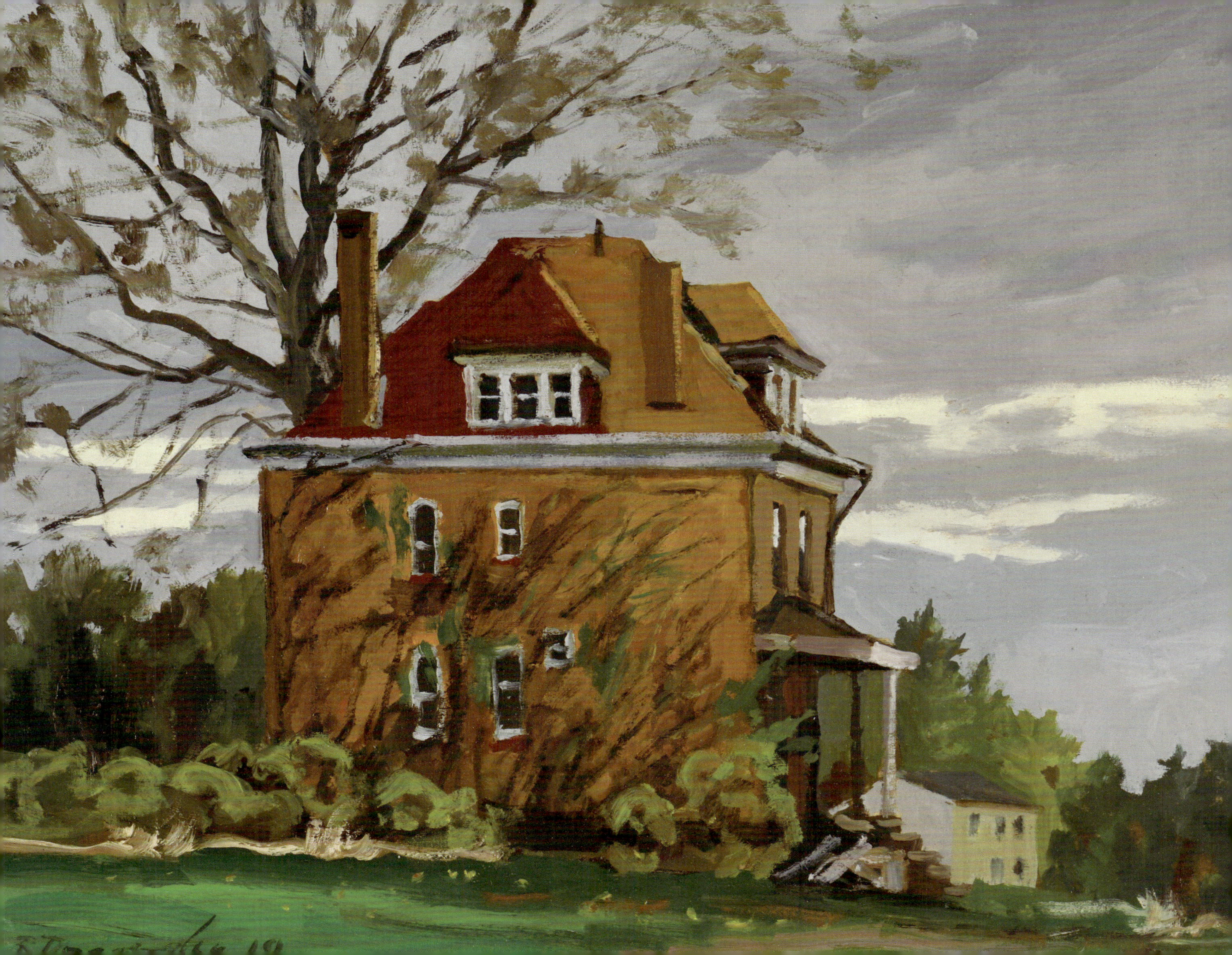

STEEL CURTAIN

West Mifflin

As I was finishing this painting, a few gentlemen approached. They were part of the construction crew for the new steel rollercoaster at Kennywood Park. They explained that the height of 220 feet was quite a climb to install the lights that weighed 90 pounds each. I quipped, "You must not be afraid of heights?"

"Actually, I don't like heights," one of the men retorted.

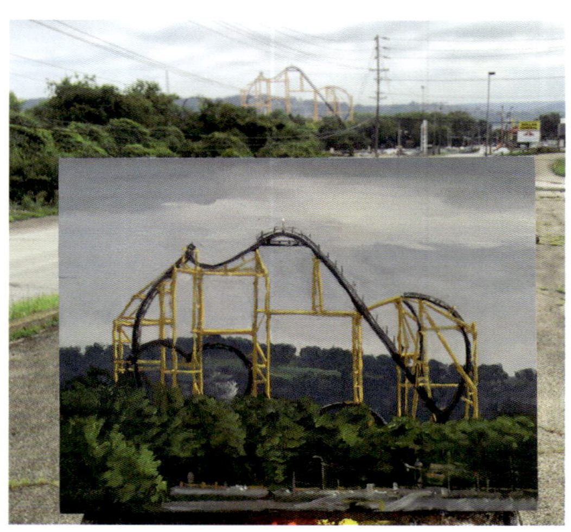

It was interesting to set up my easel near the park because it brought back good memories. I was thinking about riding the rollercoasters with my children. What a hoot!

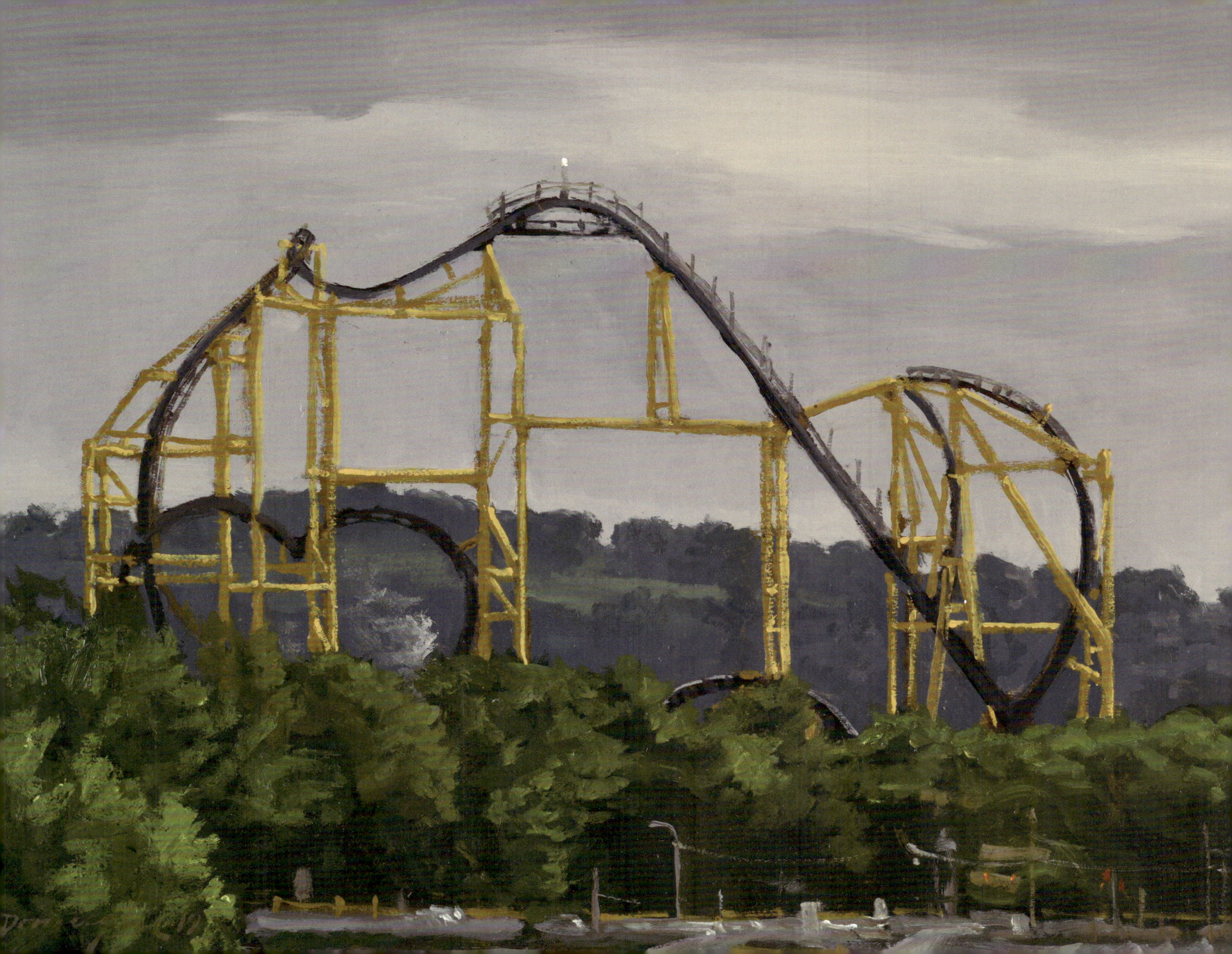

THUNDERBOLT

West Mifflin

The thrill of an amusement park resonates for a lifetime. I recently discovered a joyful photo from the early 1940s of my parents at this park. It was a surprise to know they traveled ninety-five miles to enjoy the park.

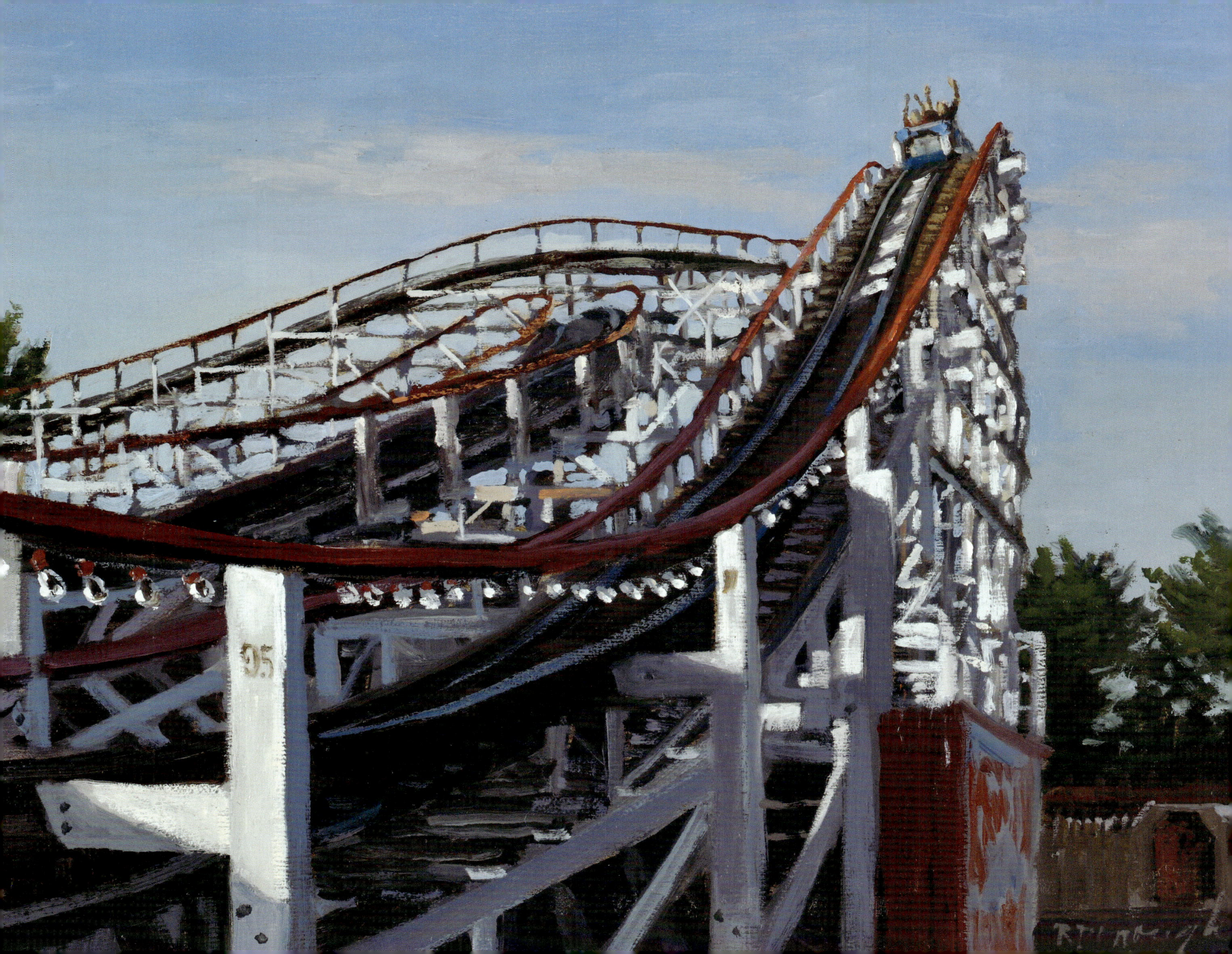

UNION RAILROAD

East Pittsburgh

The cut stone bridge supports for old railroad bridges tell quite a story of the industrial past. They were made to last and they have, functioning perfectly 150 years after construction.

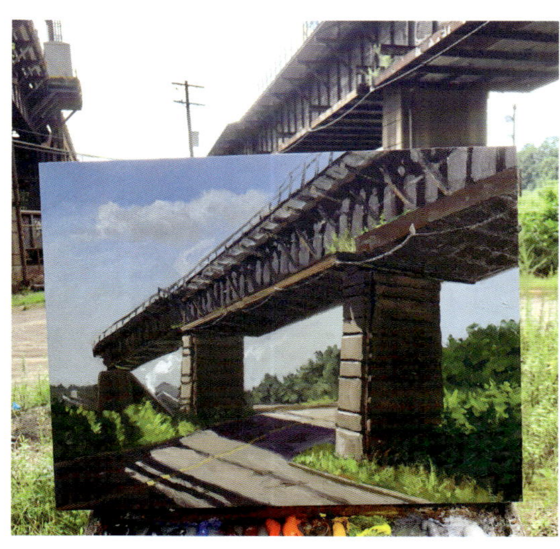

The sound of overhead trains, the sight of plumes, and the unmistakable smell of a steel mill add to the experience of being an outdoor painter.

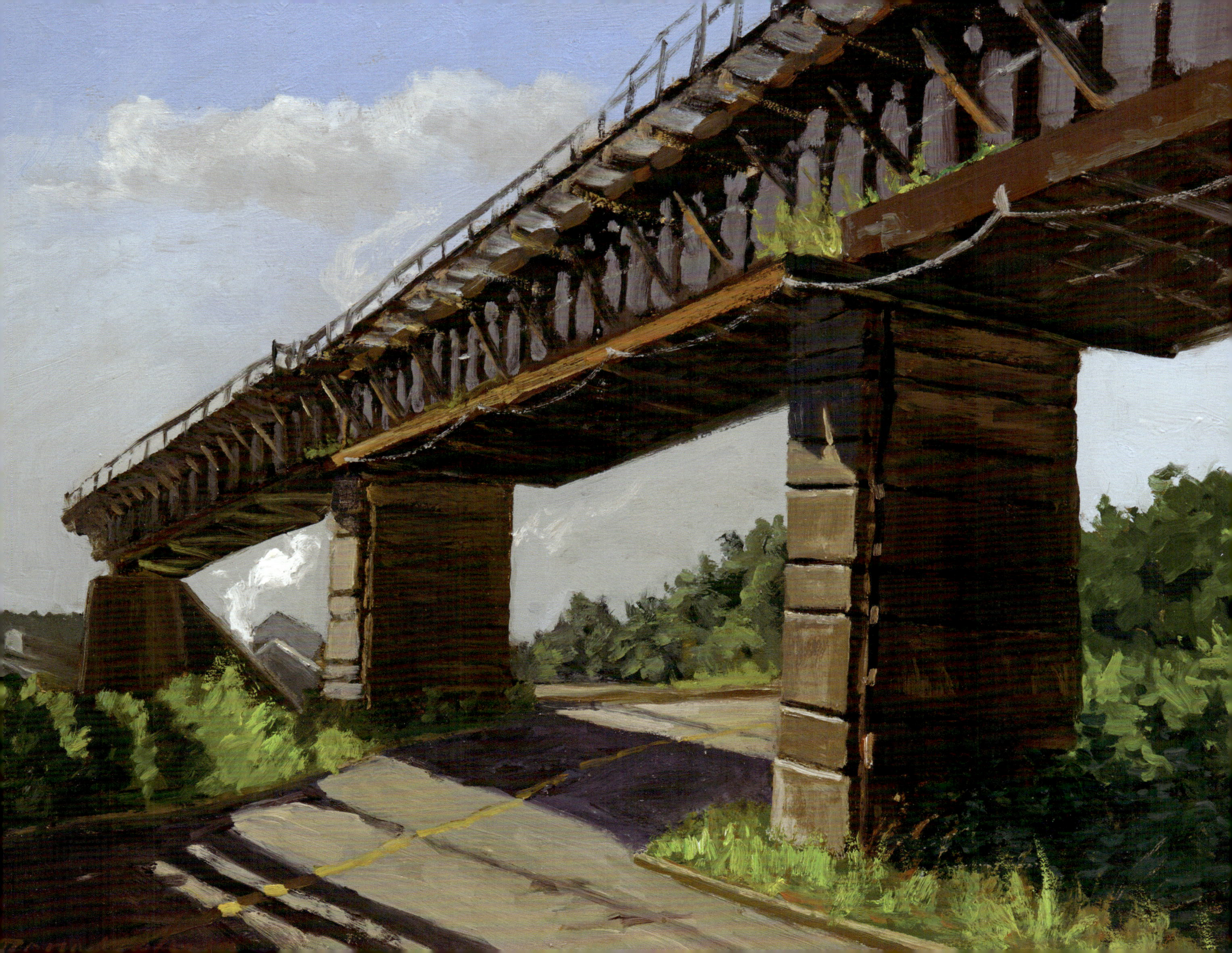

EDGAR THOMSON

Braddock

The palette of colors needed for any painting is determined by the day and the subject. Because I've been painting the Edgar Thomson Plant for many years, I've come to appreciate its subtle color shifts, which are primarily grays. A flash of fire can easily become the focal point when surrounded by gray structures, gray landscape, gray clouds, and gray plumes.

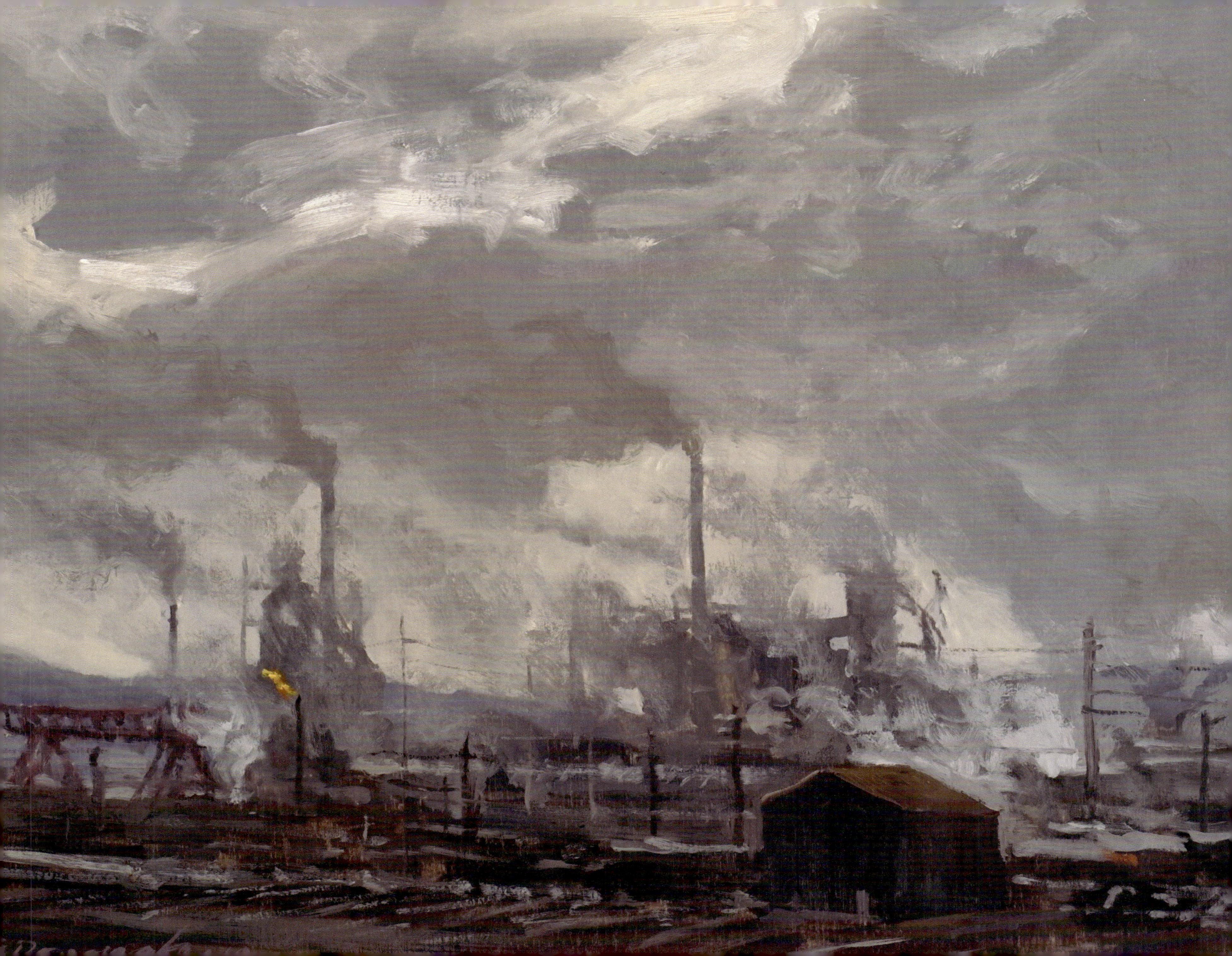

ET REFLECTION

Braddock, view from the Rankin Bridge

Painting from the Rankin Bridge was out of the question, so I held my camera out the window of my truck to capture the image. The plumes against the morning sky created a powerful scene. The Mon River current acted as a fractured mirror for the reflection.

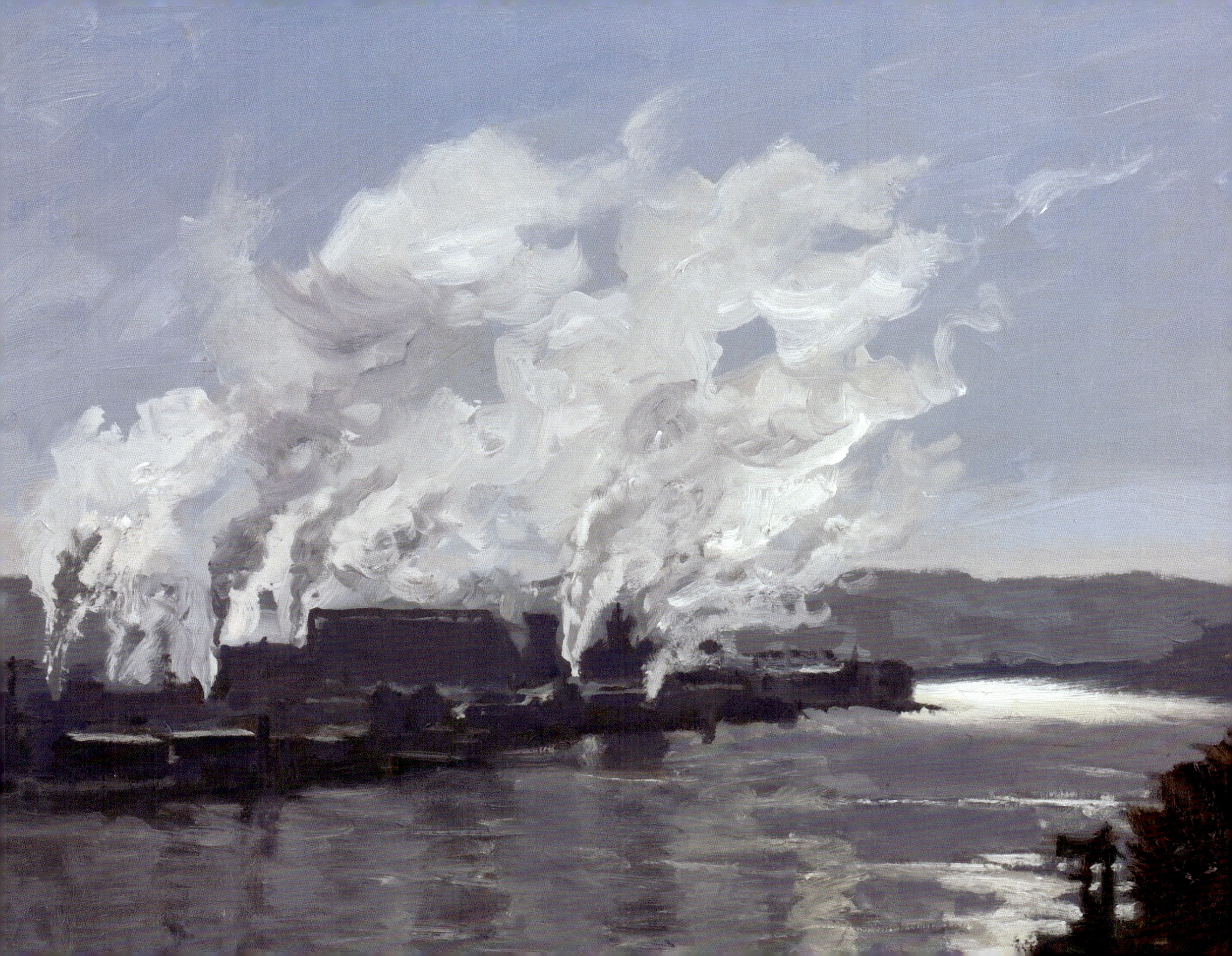

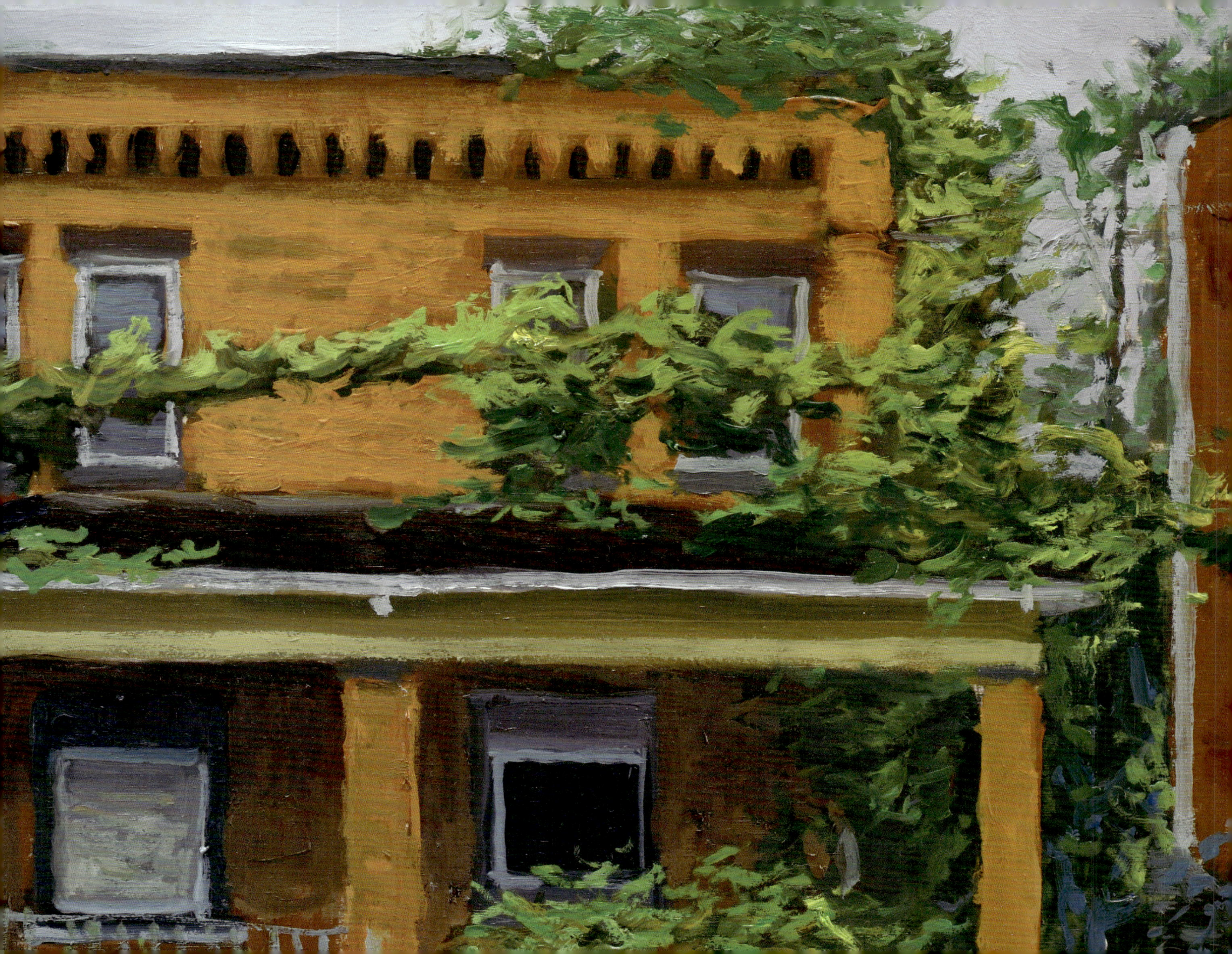

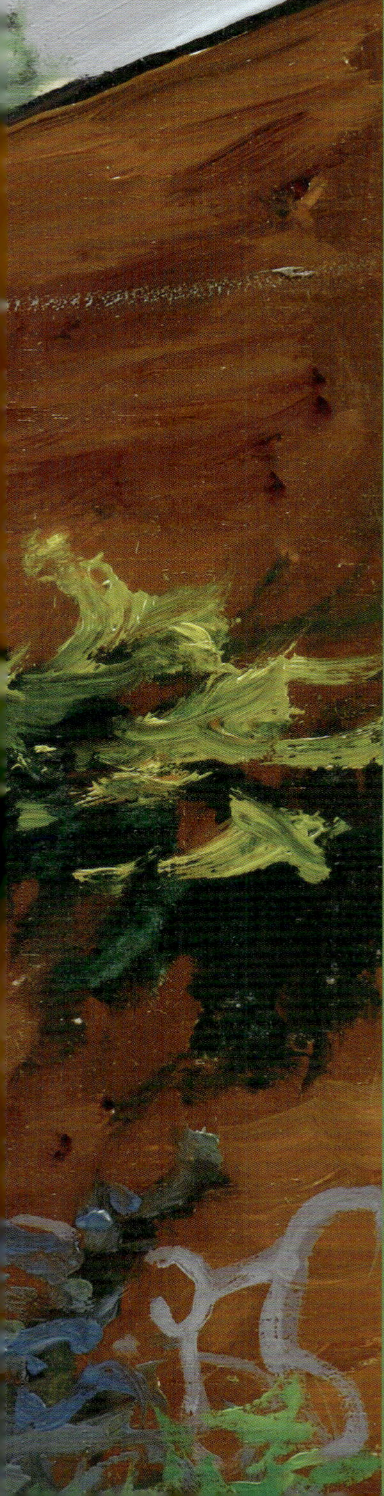

JULIUS

Julius grew up in Sharpsburg, Pennsylvania, before moving to the Mon Valley. He worked in McKeesport, which was known as "Tube City" because of the tube manufacturing in the area. He was in the Laborers' Union Local 1058 and worked for a construction company located along the river, behind the mill. He says that when the mill shut down, everything went downhill. He later worked as a mechanic for a trucking company. Now he lives in Duquesne and has many children, grandchildren, and great-grandchildren. "When the mill went down, everything went down. On a Saturday like today you could go to downtown McKeesport and you'd be arm and arm with people. After the mills shut down, people started moving out and stopped taking care of their homes."

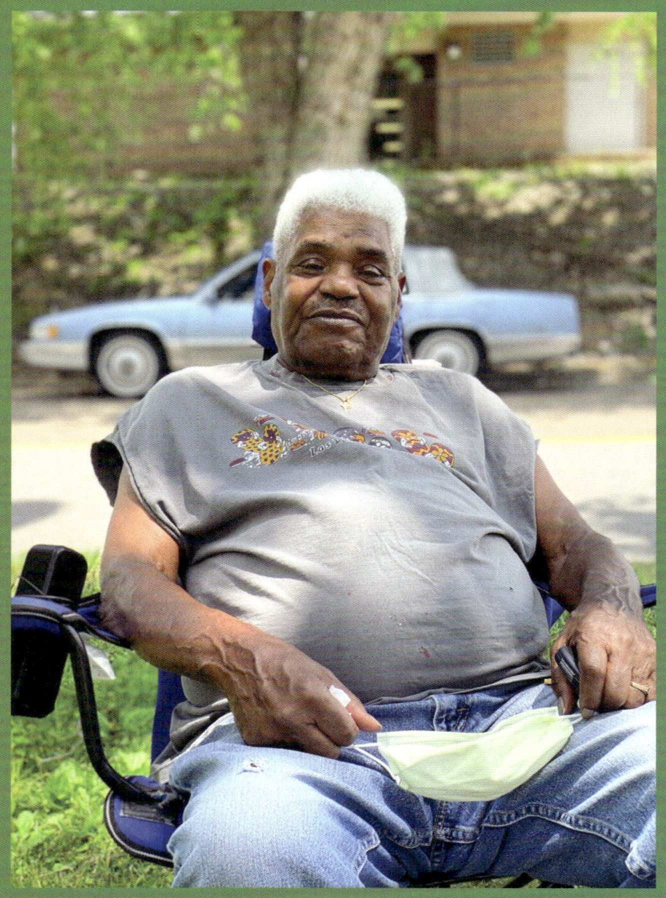

FLARE

Braddock, view from East Pittsburgh

Most paintings are started and completed on location, and on dry days. This particular day was extremely wet. The moisture enveloped the scene, making it soft and almost monochromatic. There is something beautiful about a steel mill as it operates. Seeing it from a distant high vista is like watching an industrial symphony.

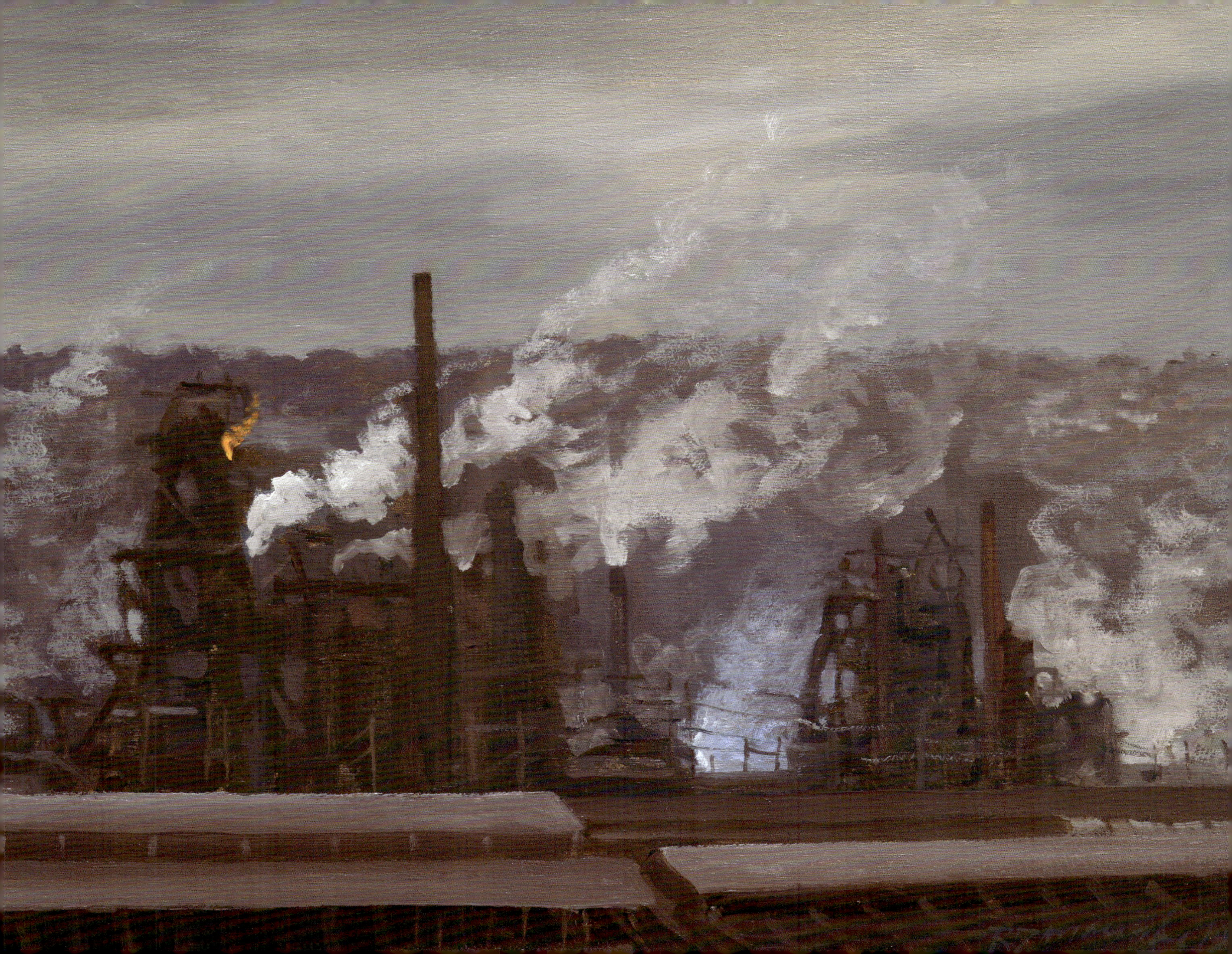

INDUSTRIAL PLUMES

Braddock

The gentle breeze plays a large part in shifting plumes. As I painted these "moving targets," I realized how they also reflect light. The cool light from the sky and the warm ground create the elegant forms.

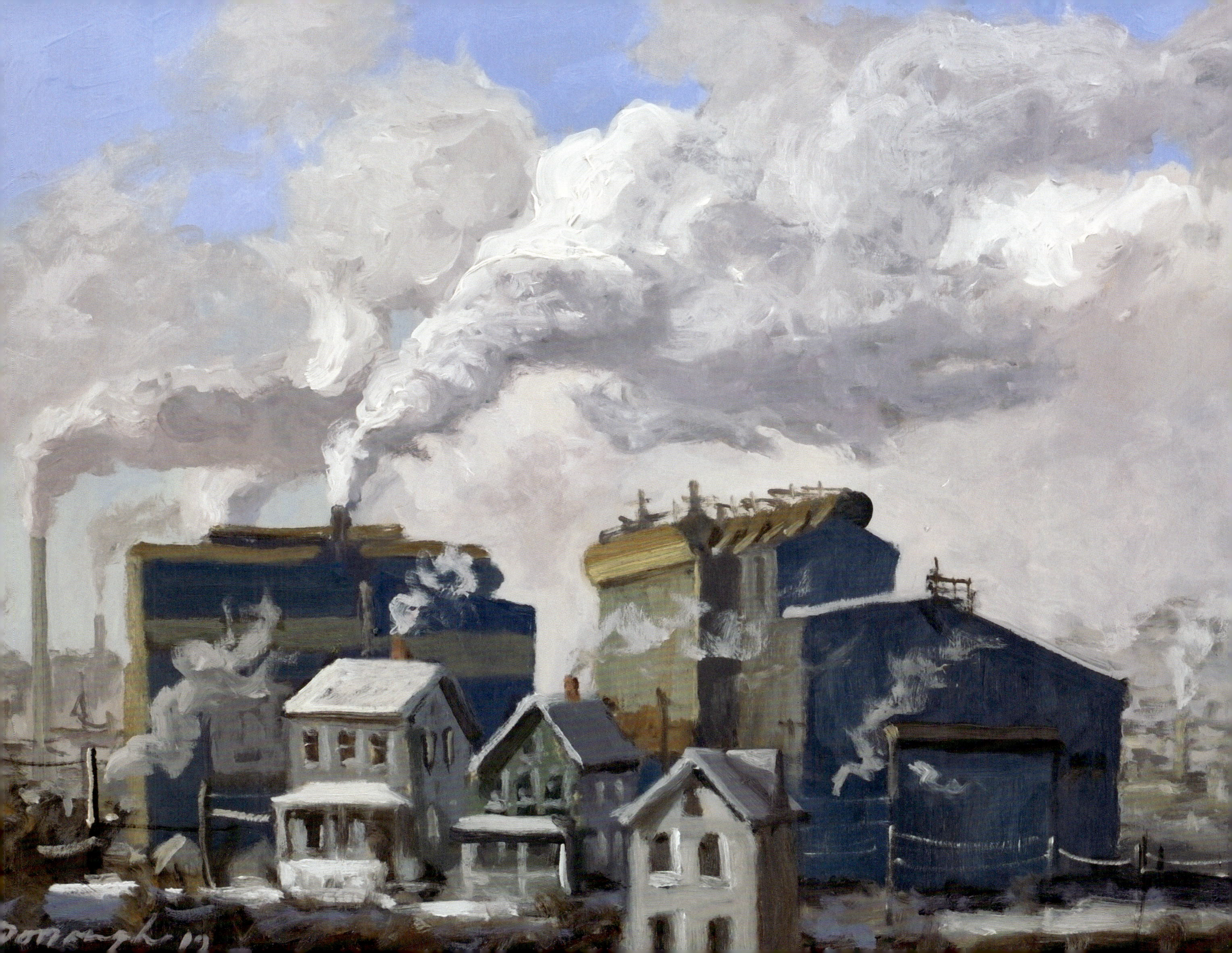

Donough '12

INDUSTRY

Braddock, view from East Pittsburgh

This painting was completed from a perch at the end of Bessemer Avenue. East Pittsburgh offers some of the best vistas of the sprawling industrial valley. This street holds special meaning because the Bessemer process allowed the first mass production of steel from molten pig iron.

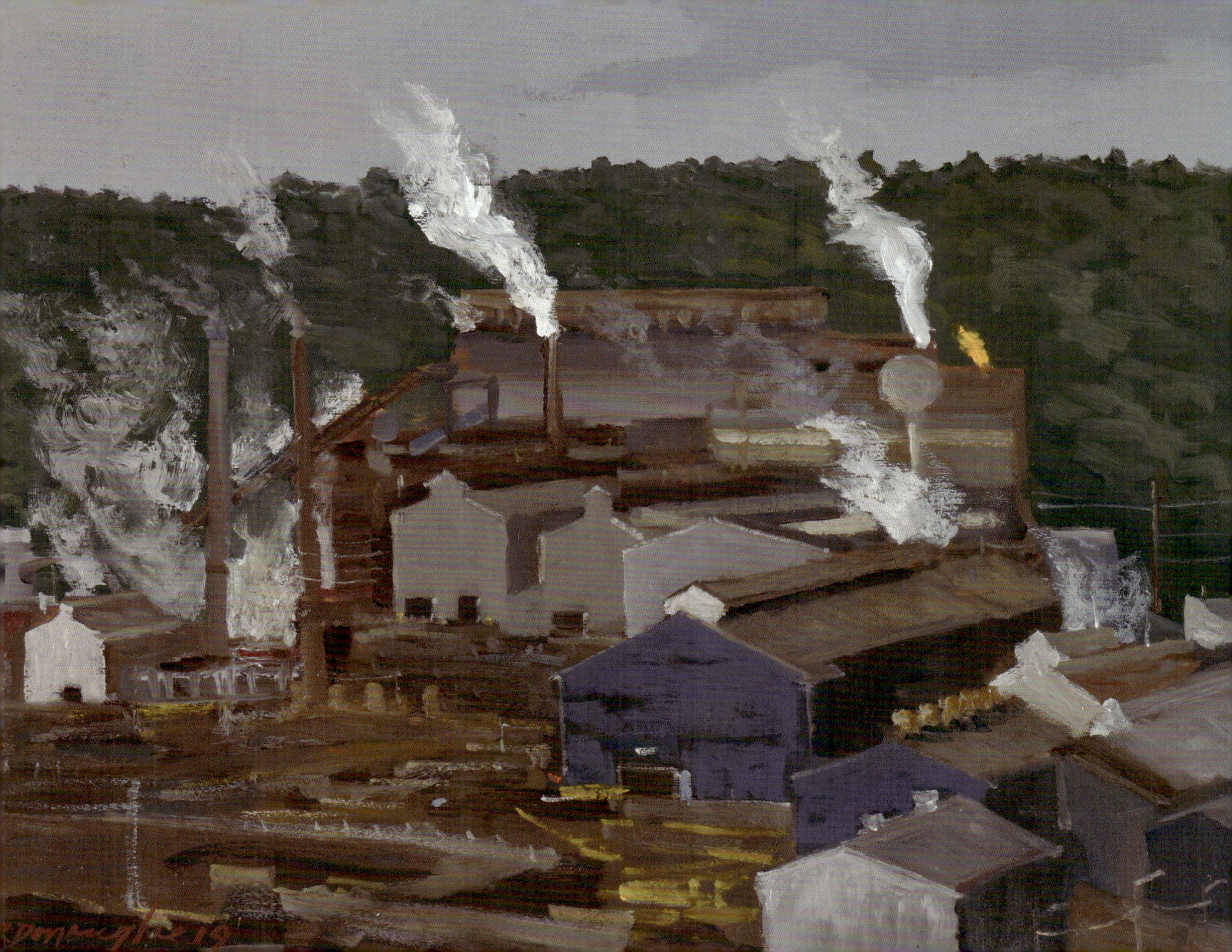
Donough '19

MON VALLEY WORKS

Braddock

This was Andrew Carnegie's first steel mill, founded in 1875. The mill appears to be a breathing industrial dragon. Plumes and flames escape from unexpected areas, giving the illusion it is alive.

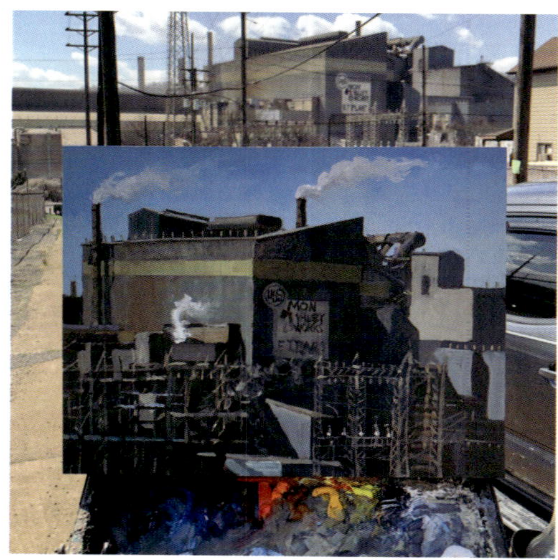

The Mon Valley Works and town of Braddock have been a favorite subject of mine for the last twenty-five years. I feel like I'm documenting an era that is slowly slipping away.

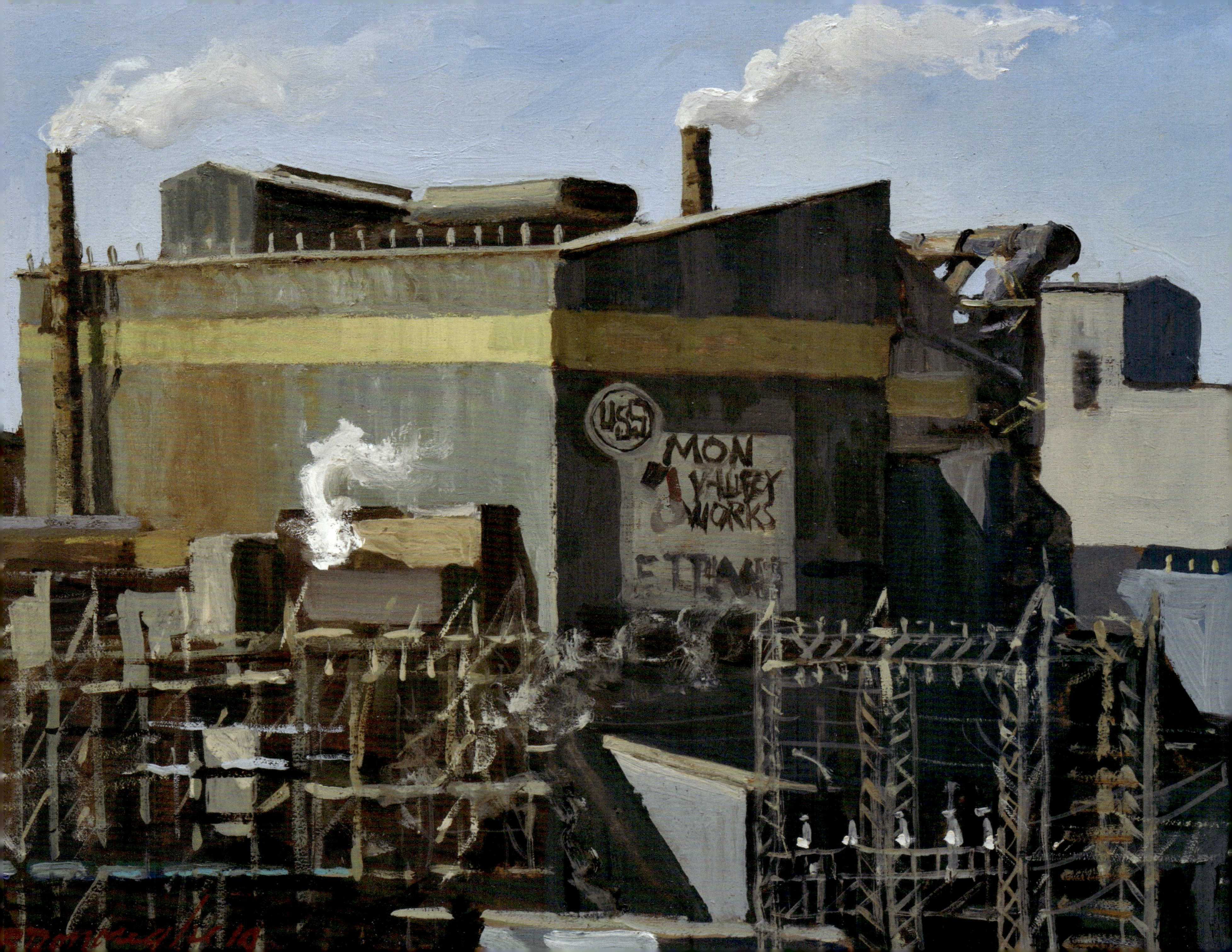
USS
MON VALLEY WORKS
ETNA

BURN OUT

North Braddock

The color harmony of this burned structure attracted me to paint it. Some scenes call out to be painted, and it's difficult sometimes to know exactly why that happens. Even though this was obviously a devastating event, I felt like it made for an intriguing piece.

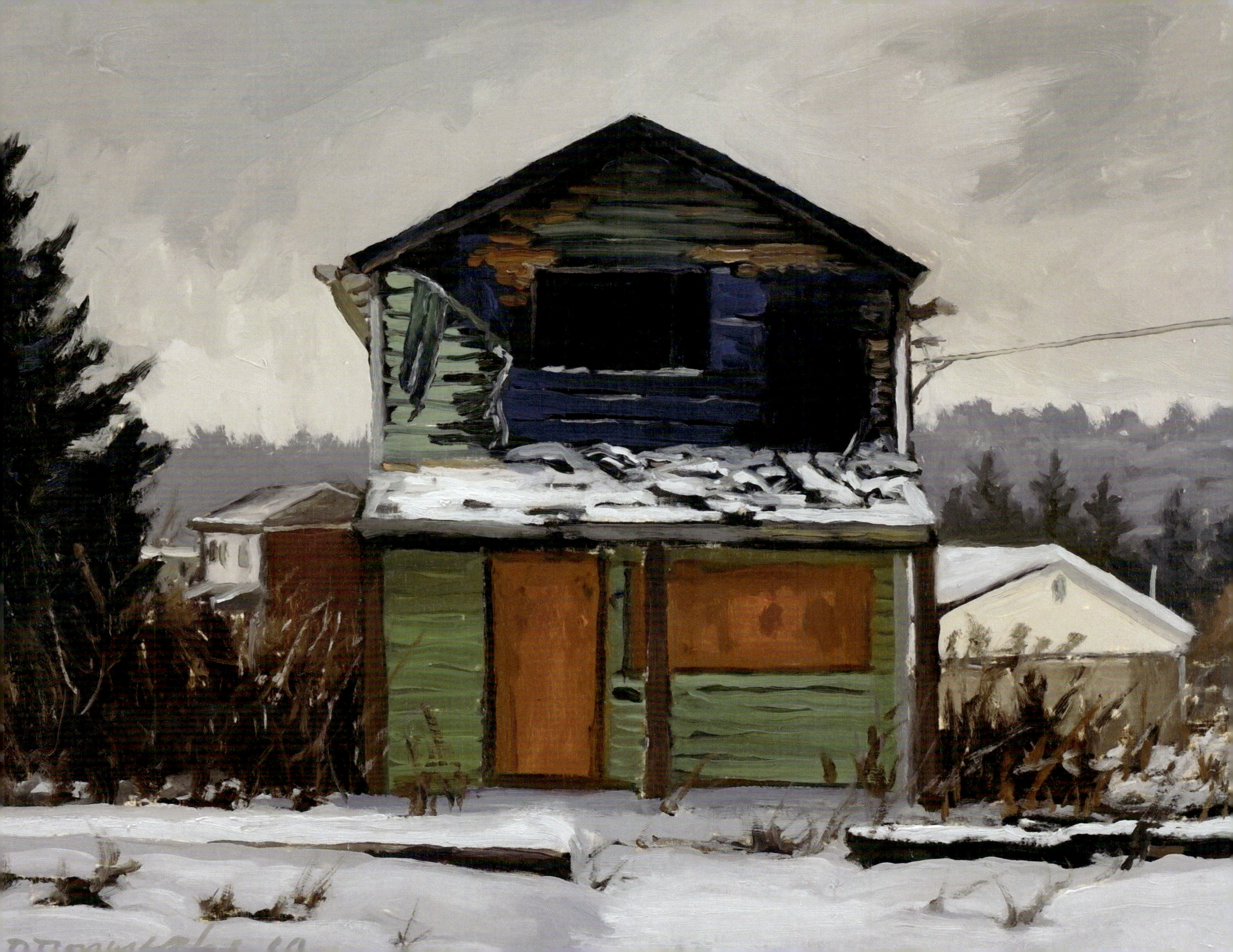

OUT OF THIS FURNACE

The novel *Out of This Furnace*, by Thomas Bell, was my inspiration to paint Braddock. In it, three generations of a Slovak family struggle to find their American dream. I painted this on location where I believe a family like the Krachas would have lived.

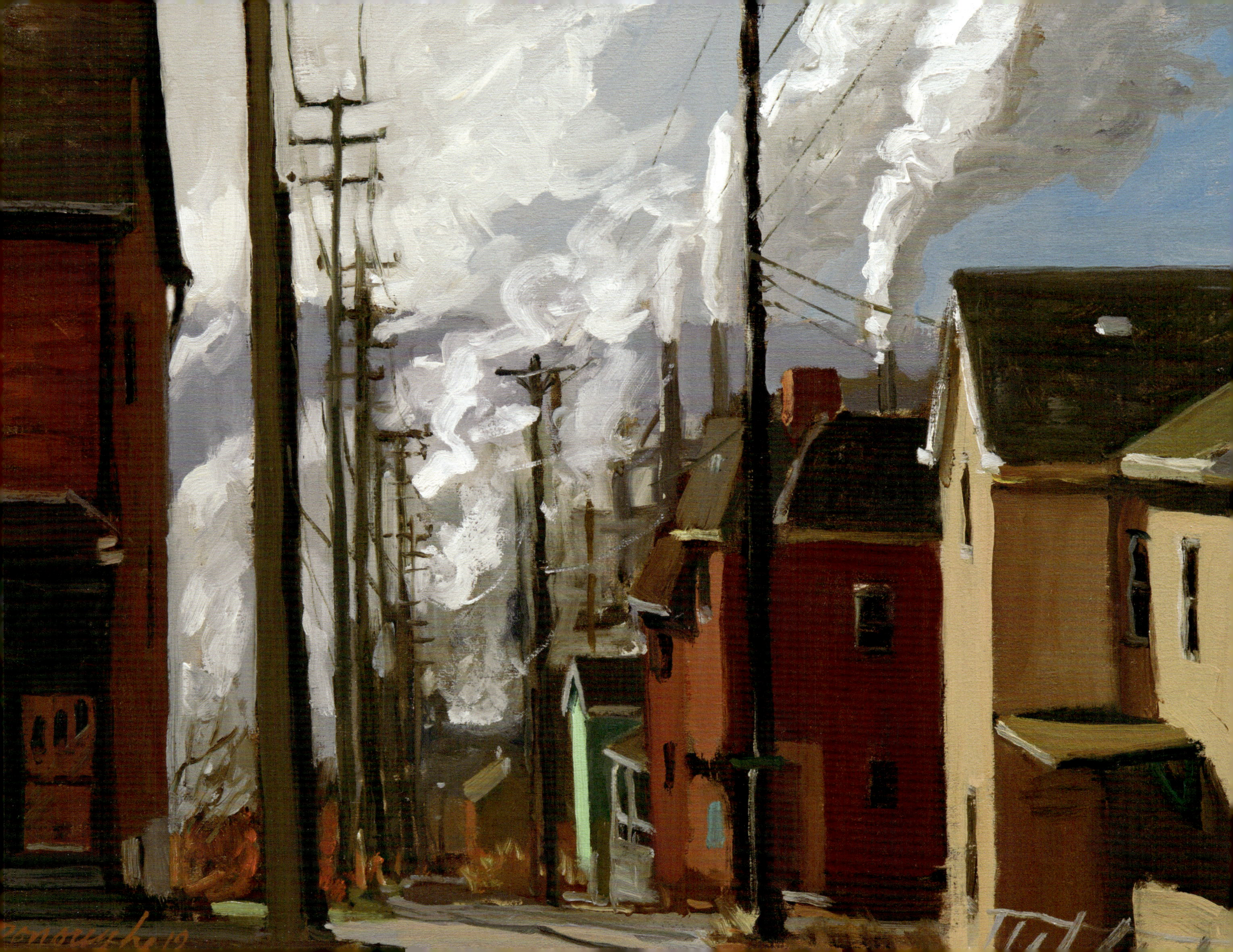

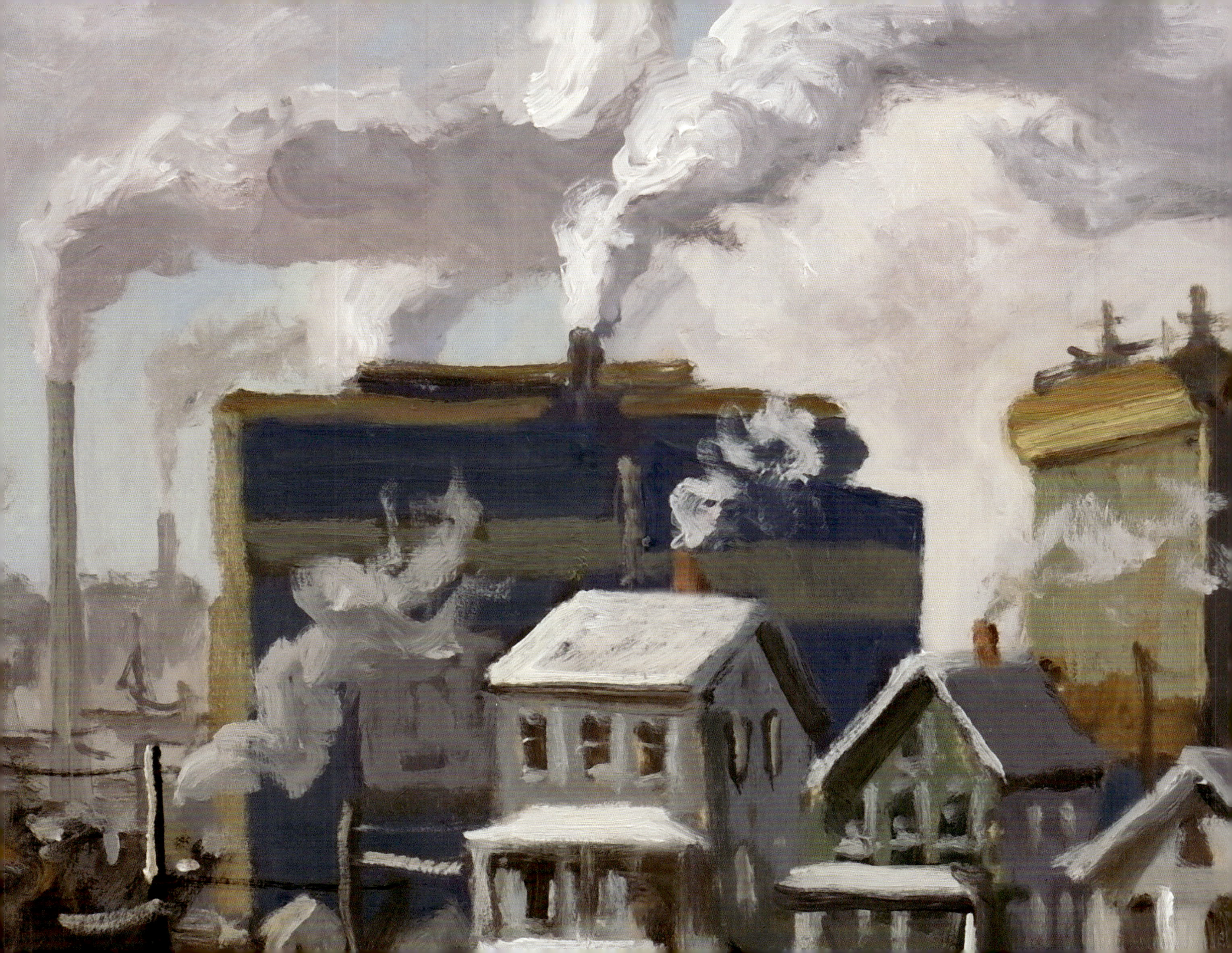

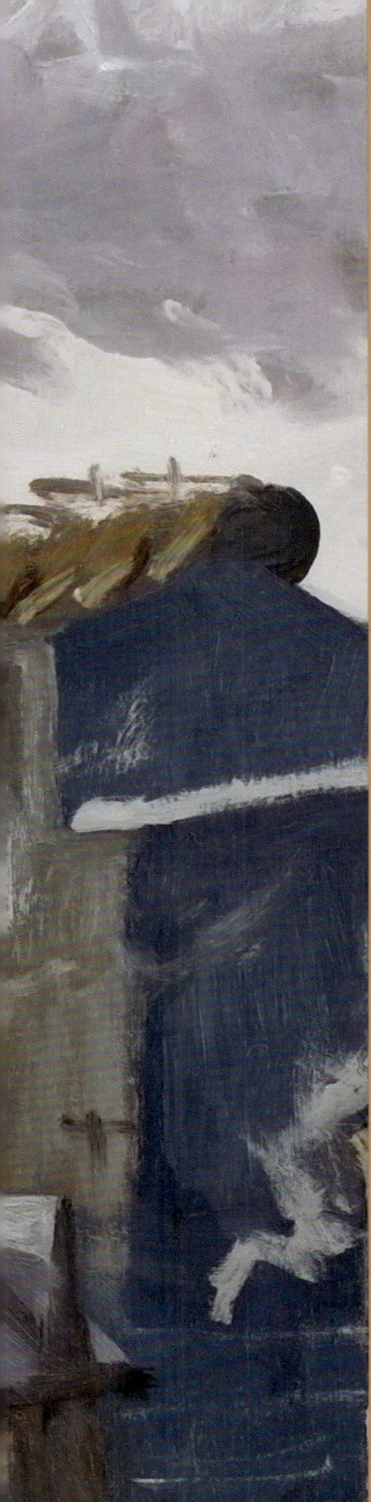

MELISSA

Melissa graduated from Woodland Hills High School in 2013 and lives with her mother now in North Braddock. The home overlooks the Mon Valley Works–Edgar Thomson Plant. She works at a restaurant and is excited about recently purchasing a car. "North Braddock is a beautiful place. The people are nice. There is a ninety-seven-year-old woman who comes out and cleans up. Everybody looks out for each other. Some of these houses have a ton of potential. The mill doesn't help it smell that great, but it's a fine place. It's fine until you have knuckleheads come around. It feels like home. It is home to me. I don't want to go away from it."

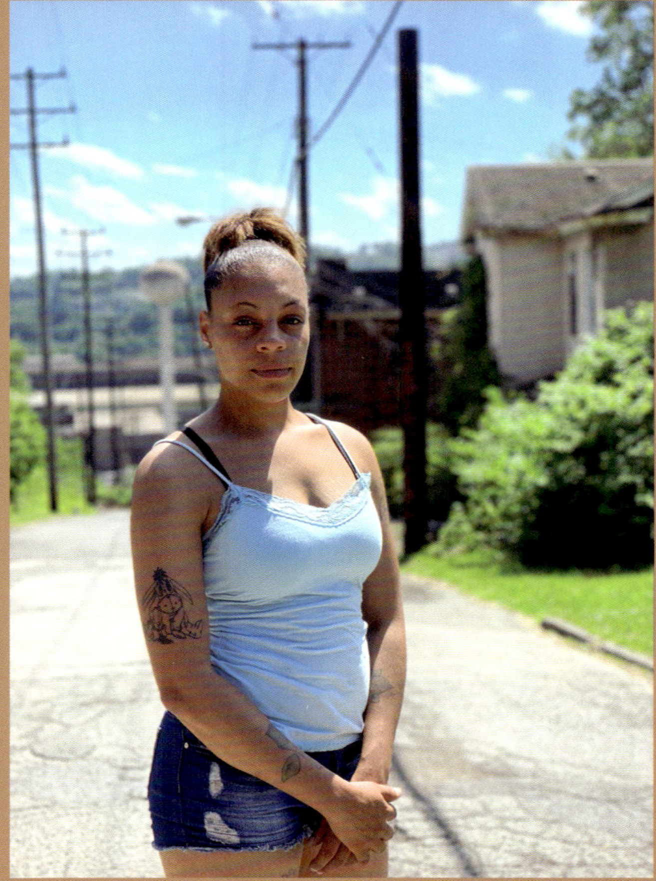

OVERTAKEN

North Braddock

As I started this project, the first thing I noticed were the abandoned homes. It is a very sad fact that many houses in the Mon Valley are not occupied. Many beautiful structures could still be rehabilitated.

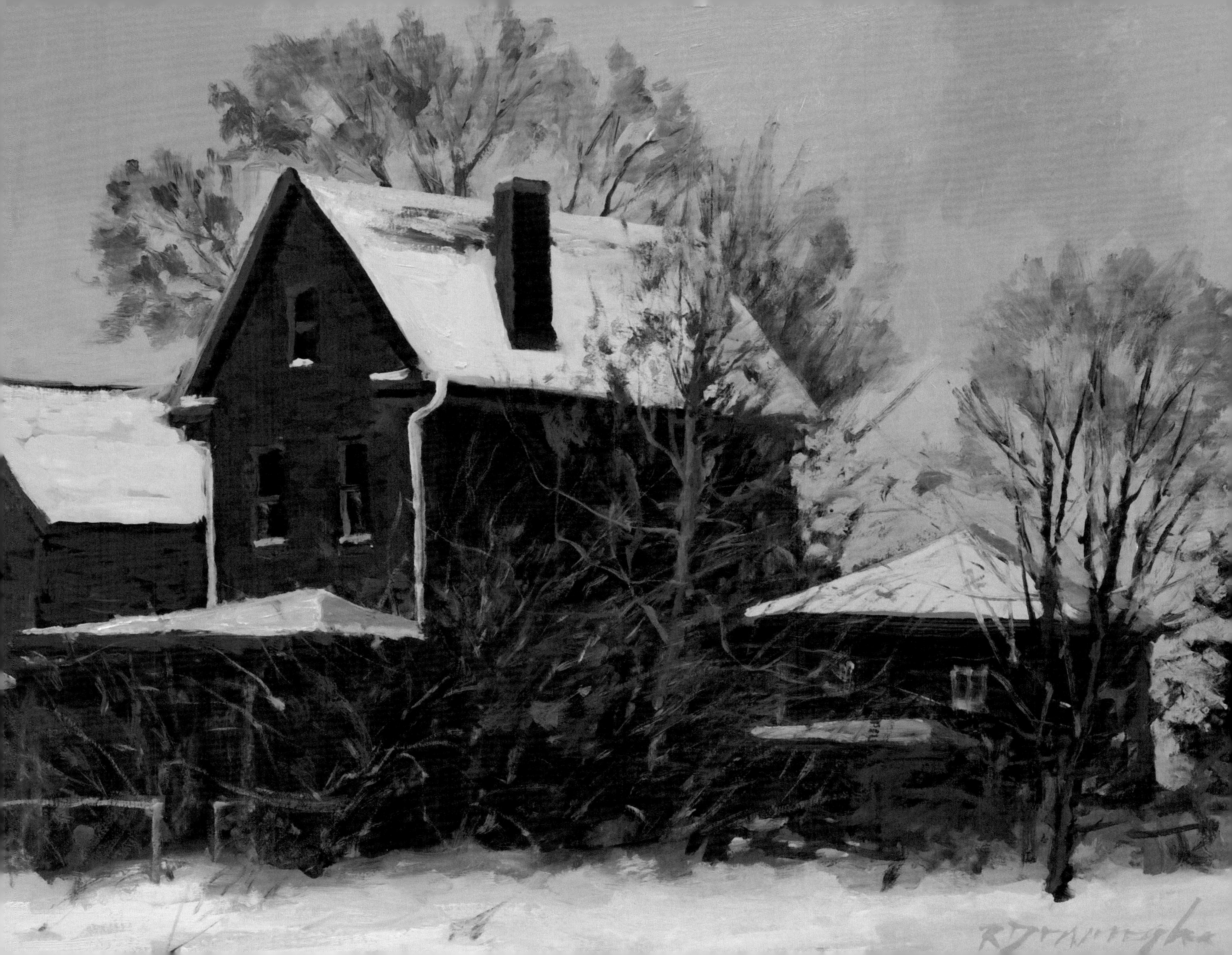

CARRIE BLAST FURNACES

These iron furnaces, which were built in 1907, stand today as a monument to the great age of iron production in Pennsylvania. They are on the National Register of Historic Places and can be visited. It's a rare opportunity to see how iron was produced at this site until 1978.

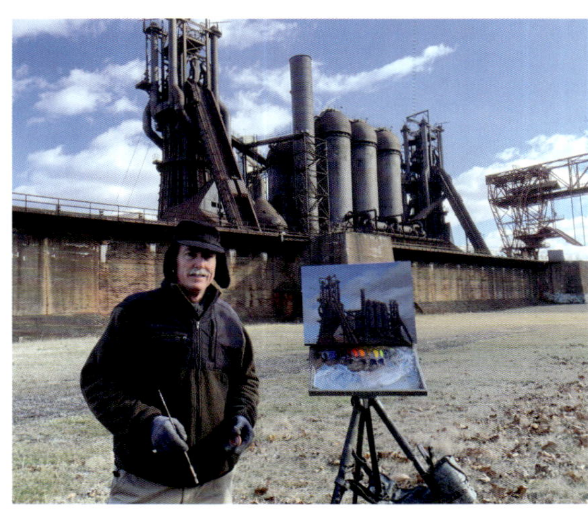

The nice folks from Rivers of Steel allowed me to visit and paint. I'm photographed by Ron Baraff, director of Historic Resources and Facilities.

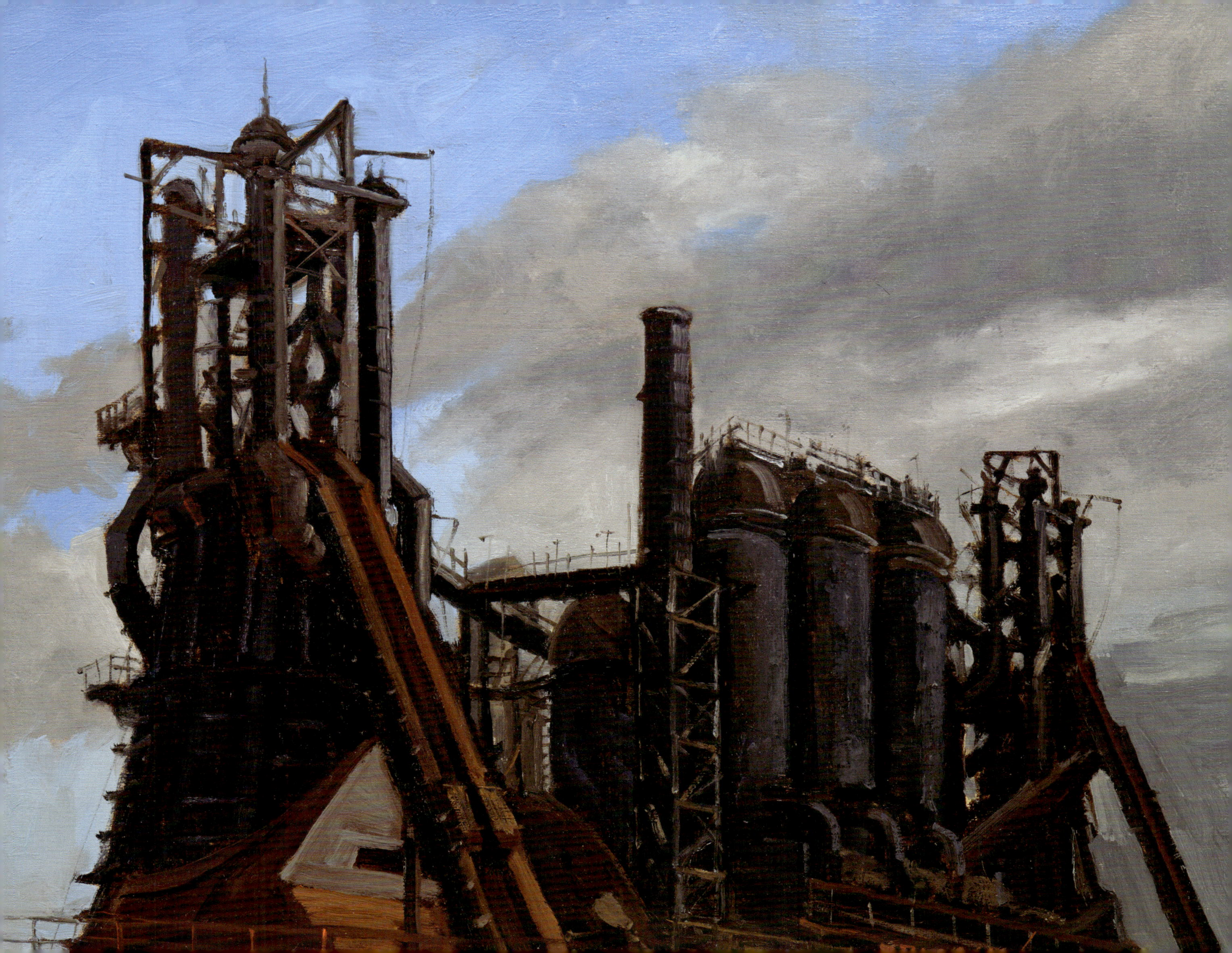

AFTERWORD

The Persistence of Memory and Spirit

COMMUNITIES ARE ROOTED IN THE PERSISTENCE OF MEMORY. There is a deep-seated connection between a people, their past, and their environs. We collectively utilize this persistence as the driving force for our attachment to "place" and employ it for rediscovery and rebirth. We are grounded in who we are as a region by our past—glorious and inglorious; success and failure; triumph and tragedy—all form the basis of our identity. The disparate communities that make up the rich "Valley of Decision" resonate with the spirit and memory of the past.

The majesty and dominance of the valley towns lie in their essence, within their stories, their peoples, and their spirit. The boom times brought blossoming success and promise fostered in innovation, hard work, dedication, and a pious belief that the American Dream was real and achievable. Among the backdrop of the mills and mines, communities grew, echoing the call of the burgeoning American twentieth century as the region transformed itself into an industrial powerhouse providing goods, opportunity, and thousands of jobs for those who lived here and those who flocked into the region from the Old World and the American South.

Rivers of Steel has worked with the many communities throughout the region. Our mission is to showcase the artistry and innovation of our region's industrial and cultural heritage through its historical and twenty-first-century attractions—offering unique experiences via tours, workshops, exhibitions, festivals, and more.

It is against the backdrop of our mission that we work throughout the heritage area to form partnerships and collations. The opportunity to work with Ron Donoughe and his Mon Valley project was one that dovetailed with our efforts to showcase the region. His work encapsulates our mission—the drive to tell the story of the area and its rich fabric of interwoven stories and experiences. We welcomed the chance, knowing that his vision, his lens, and his brushstrokes would create a picture of the valley that echoes its depth, beauty, complexity, and resolve. It is from among these hills and hollows that our region reaches out to beyond our boundaries . . . we as a people have created a world in which our place is central. Through ingenuity, innovation, and hard work, the Mon Valley has shaped an indelible place within the American memory. Just as our triumphs have inspired and influenced, our tragedies and struggles have taken their place center stage as we work to right ourselves and discover not just who we were but who we are and who we want to be moving forward.

We are strong yet scarred. We are resilient yet cautious. Up and down the valley we endeavor to find our footing and identity. We know we can and will triumph if we work together. Projects such as Ron's help to bridge the gaps that exist within and between these communities. It shows us to be far more similar in spirit than not and that despite our differences we share a memory of our past and a vision of our future. We are survivors, persistent and resolute. Through our collective efforts, and through the arts and investment, the valley can and will survive into the twenty-first century. Memory and spirit will persevere . . .

— RON BARAFF
Director of Historic Resources & Facilities, Rivers of Steel

ACKNOWLEDGMENTS

THIS PROJECT, *BROWNSVILLE TO BRADDOCK*, HAS BEEN PERCOLATING for some time. But it likely would not have happened without the gentle encouragement of someone close to me. Catherine Berard's grandparents lived in Monessen and she spent much of her childhood there. It was her memories that prompted me to explore a region that was calling out to be my next painting project. On January 1, 2019, the project commenced as we made our first trip to Brownsville and began exploring the river towns north to Braddock.

It was one of those "build it and they will come" moments. And, since the world sometimes seems to conspire to help with projects created from a passionate heart, many people came forward to offer assistance. Dean Simpson and Travis Winters from Touchstone Center for Crafts connected me to Pamela Twiss, Maggy Aston, and Barbara Engle at California University of Pennsylvania and also to Chris McGinnis and Ron Baraff from Rivers of Steel. Ron contributed the afterword, "The Persistence of Memory and Spirit." Both organizations offered to host the exhibition and help with publicity. Sandy Crooms and John Fagan from the University of Pittsburgh Press expressed a sincere interest early in the project. Cathy McCollum and Wendy Duchene from the Mon River Towns Program assisted, as did Donna Holdorf from the National Road Heritage Corridor.

Max King, who recently published *The Good Neighbor: The Life and Work of Fred Rogers*, was kind enough to write the foreword. The Robert S. Waters Fund at the Pittsburgh Foundation, Bruce Zewe, and Mark and Marsha Bookman helped with moral and financial support. Lynne Glover offered her watchful eye for thoughtful edits. Ric Evans and his son Luke carefully reproduced the images for this publication. My son Seth created the map and provided valuable feedback on the project as it progressed. Beau Berman accompanied me to the Mon Valley and assisted with interviews and videos.

I cannot thank everyone enough.

— RON DONOUGHE